HOW TO
PREPARE
AND
DELIVER

Dynamic
Presentations

HOW TO PREPARE AND DELIVER

Dynamic
Presentations

Andrew E. Schwartz

WHOLE PERSON ASSOCIATES
Duluth, Minnesota

Whole Person Associates, Inc.
210 West Michigan
Duluth MN 55802-1908 218-727-0500
E-mail: books@wholeperson.com
Web site: http://www.wholeperson.com

How to Prepare and Deliver Dynamic Presentations

Printed in the United States of America

10 9 8 7 6 5 4 3 2 1

Editorial Director: Susan Gustafson
Art Director: Joy Dey
Manuscript Editor: Kathy DeArmond
Production Coordinator: Paul Hapy

Library of Congress Cataloging in Publication Data

Schwartz, Andrew E.
  How to prepare and deliver dynamic presentations / Andrew E. Schwartz
  160 p. 27 cm.
  Includes bibliographical references and index.
  ISBN 1-57025-167-3 (pbk.)
  1. Training—Handbooks, manuals, etc. I. Title.
  LB1027.47 .S38 1998
   331.25'92—ddc21   98-8935
                                                    CIP

They say that the greatest fear in the world is public speaking.

This book is dedicated to all the teachers and trainers willing to deliver the goods.

In memory of my father

Table of Contents

Acknowledgments

Jacques Oury, an advertising creative, has developed and edited several works for A.E. Schwartz & Associates, including *Guided Imagery for Groups,* a Whole Person publication. Jacques lives in western Montana, where he has conceptualized and written award-winning print and broadcast ads for an array of national clients. Carla Dropo is a technical writer who has been affiliated on a consulting basis with A.E. Schwartz & Associates for several years. She is currently employed with a linguistic software company in Boston, Massachusetts. Putri L.M. Rivai is an intern beginning her affiliation with A.E. Schwartz & Associates. Last and definitely, once again to the entire staff at Whole Person Associates.

A heartfelt appreciation to our associates and interns. Special thanks to the following for their various roles and involvement over the years: Putri L.M. Rivai, Ida Faber, Melanie K. O'Donnell, Kate Steinbuhler, Dawn Packer, Christina Neamtu, Alison Crehan, Anosha Lewis, Michele Carletti, Susan Berstein, Lynn Feldman, Lisa Bell, Rob Schuller, Dan Flynn, Ben Crosson, Tim Howland, Amy, Henriette, Alissa, Adam, Anne, Marty, and "both" Bernie Rotberg's.

Applause goes to our clients, participants, and the organizations for whom I have provided management training, development, and consulting services.

Years of practical experience have led to the development of this book and many others yet to be written.

About the author

Andrew E. Schwartz is president of A.E. Schwartz & Associates of Watertown, Massachusetts, a comprehensive organization which offers over forty management and professional development training programs with workbooks and practical solutions to organizational problems (http://www.aeschwartz.com). Mr. Schwartz conducts over one hundred programs annually for clients in industry, research, technology, government, Fortune 100/500 companies, and nonprofit organizations worldwide. He is often found at conferences as a keynote presenter and/or facilitator. His style is fast-paced, participatory, practical, succinct, and enjoyable. He has taught and lectured at over a dozen colleges and universities throughout the United States.

Over 100 articles on management, professional development, and training have appeared in publications such as: *Executive Excellence* (The Institute for Principle Centered Leadership, UT); *The Director*—The Magazine for Decision Makers in Business (ABC, England); *Training*—The Magazine for Human Resource Development (Lakewood Publishers, MN); *Data Training* and *Training News* (Weingarten, Inc., MA); *Management Solutions, Entrepreneurial Excellence,* and *Trainer's Workshop* (American Management Association (AMA, NY); *Training Tools* (NCR Corporation, SC); *Meeting Manager* (Meeting Planners International, TX); *Managing* (Mirror-Times, NY); *The Non-Profit News* (The Non-Profit World, WI); *News Track Executive Tape Service* (Managers' Edge, CO); *Tools of the Trade* (New Jersey Bell, NJ); *CPA Journal* (Society of Certified Public Accountants, NY); *Management News* (National Starch, NC); *Tips for Managing* (Federal Reserve Board, DC); *Management Digest* (AP Allied Publications, FL); *The Boston Herald* (MA); *Business Worcester* (MA); and others.

Books/works include: *Delegating Authority* published by Barron's Educational Services and Cassell Publishers (U.K.); *How to Prepare and Deliver Dynamic Presentations, Guided Imagery for Groups,* and *Inquire Within* published by Whole Person Associates; *School for Managers* (6 hour audio with eighty page reference guide) published by A.E. Schwartz & Associates; *Career Essentials for Secretaries and Administrative Assistants* tape series produced by the American Management Association (AMA); *Creative Problem Solving* (2nd Ed.) workbook/tape series (AMA); *Stress Management* (2nd Ed.) a University Extension

Course (AMA); pending titles include: *Time Management* and *The Performance Management System.*

Products/reviewed and developed: 14 titles for AMA's *Business Success Series* which include: *Speaking & Listening Skills, Practical Problem Solving Skills, Negotiating Skills, Developing Your Leadership Skills, How to Learn: Successful Strategies, Self-Esteem: Building a Positive Attitude, Developing Basic Job Skills, How to Think Creatively, Interpersonal Communication Skills, How to Build Team Skills, Enhancing Reading Efficiency,* and *Motivation/Goal Setting.* Developed and wrote documentation for TR-PLUS (computer software which allows for the total administrative automation of an organization's entire training department's needs).

Overview

This manual will take novice trainers through the fundamentals of a classroom-style training program, from program design to development to implementation. It will provide them with real-life examples of the training process. More experienced trainers will use this manual to assess their strengths and limitations. Seasoned trainers will find the specific tips, clearly defined techniques, and worksheets extremely useful when they train other trainers. This manual may also be used as a resource book for educators who teach courses in training and development. Finally, even if you are not teaching a formal class or program, you will benefit from learning the kind of skills described on the following pages.

The worksheets included in each section allow you to practice these newly acquired skills that are necessary to become a dynamic and effective trainer. The hundreds of examples included—drawn from years of experience in the preparation and delivery of training programs—will help you make the leap from theory to practice. And since life often does not "go by the book," we offer suggestions in case our training techniques go awry.

Welcome

Welcome to *How to Prepare and Deliver Dynamic Presentations,* a skills-oriented, interactive manual designed with you in mind.

You are human resource specialists and corporate trainers, health care professionals and educators, counselors and consultants, team leaders and project leaders.

You are people who lead and guide adults in their pursuit of knowledge and new skills, and even in relearning old skills.

You are responsible for helping others to learn.

How to use our format

This manual is designed to give you the most user-friendly, step-by-step and skill-by-skill tour on how to create an effective training program. In Chapter One we will familiarize you with the traits of the adult learner. Adult learners approach training—especially when it resembles a classroom situation—with the knowledge and confidence that they're not children and should not be talked down to. It takes more credibility and effort to teach adults. Their bases of knowledge are wide and their mental filters are usually working full-time.

Chapter Two broadens your newly acquired knowledge of adult learners and guides you through the design and development phases of a training program. In this highly interactive chapter you'll learn to analyze your group of learners, prepare a teaching plan, write performance goals, and design a program that matches your learners' profiles.

And finally, Chapter Three applies the steps and skills included in an effective training program to the actual delivery. In this chapter we'll focus on YOU, the facilitator, and how you can take the knowledge of your audience, combined with the knowledge of your program, and make it all mesh. We'll help you determine your personal style and let you use it effectively. You'll have an inventory list of facilitator skills to refer to, and a final checklist to ensure you apply all these skills effectively.

Each of these three chapters is organized in a lesson/exercise/review format, and contains visuals, guides, and summaries.

You also have a study partner, Ruth, whom you will meet soon.

You can use this manual in a variety of ways, depending on your needs. Although these chapters work best as a unit, each one can stand alone, specifically for those only interested in learning about adult learners, only needing to design an effective program, or only interested in delivering training material more effectively.

More experienced trainers will also find the step-by-step process of this book to be an effective tool for training. You may find some of the information remedial and simplistic; the groups you work with definitely will not. This manual will then become a rich reference guide for quick training tips.

Exactly how will you learn?

Throughout the manual we will ask you to think about and focus on your own learning process. Answering the following questions will help you become more attentive to the learning dynamics of your trainees.

- What exercises did you respond well to?

- Which ones do you have trouble remembering?

- How does it feel to be a student?

To help you get acquainted with some of our terminology, write down your definitions for these terms: trainer, facilitator, coach, mentor, and instructor.

Think about which of these roles you have already filled. You may not be aware of it, but you already have some teaching skills because you have held at least one of these positions—at least informally. As a parent, perhaps you taught your teenage children to drive. At work you may have mentored new colleagues, helping them to learn their job. And as adults, most of us, at one time or another, have coached a friend through a difficult personal situation.

Now that you've explored your experiences as a teacher, let's switch roles. Even if you have never taken a continuing education class or attended a formal training program, you certainly know what it feels like to be an adult student/learner. We have all had to learn new skills at home (how to fix a leaky faucet, trim a turkey, or burp a baby) and master new skills at work (a word-processing program, for example). We develop new interpersonal skills when we learn how to get along with a difficult colleague or to accommodate a friend whose style is different from our own.

And now that you've tried on both shoes—first as a teacher and then as an adult learner—think about how you behaved in each role and what you felt. Did you enjoy teaching? Was it satisfying? Frustrating? What did you do specifically that enabled your "student" to learn successfully? Looking back, can you think of anything you could have done to improve the learning situation?

Now think of a moment when you were a learner. What did your "teachers" do to help you to learn? Did they behave in any ways which hindered your learning? Were your teachers able to create an environment in which you felt safe to take risks and make mistakes? Were you stimulated by the learning situation? How was information presented effectively or ineffectively?

The answers to these questions are what you bring to the training situation. Of course, if you have no answers, whether from lack of experience or inability to remember, relax. This book offers possible solutions and approaches.

Now meet Ruth, your study partner

We try to teach by example, so throughout the course of this volume you will have a study partner.

Ruth is head of personnel and human resources at Arlee County Hospital, a privately funded institution serving a district of 5 small towns, amounting to about 30,000 residents. "A.C.," as it is known to everyone, employs about 250 full-time staffers (from janitors to orderlies to nurses to administrational personnel such as Ruth herself) and is steered by a 12 member board of directors, whose chairperson also serves as hospital president. Her name is Alissa.

Alissa recently charged Ruth with the difficult task of creating, designing, planning, and facilitating a mandatory stress-management program for the hospital's staff of 40 nurses.

> About half the nurses are registered nurses (R.N.'s), and the remaining half are either volunteer health care workers with Americorps or midwives-in-training enrolled at a local midwifery facility. It's a mixed bag, and I realized that one specific approach may not have worked for all of them.

Three head nurses (Amy, Henriette, and Adam) are Ruth's main sources, "contact points" who helped her get a handle on how their staff deals with many stressful situations, such as difficulties between conventional medicine and a growing demand for midwives, gender differences between a mostly female nursing staff and younger male orderlies (or older male surgeons), and of course trauma cases. A.C. is home to the county's largest and most complete trauma facility; in an urban county with heavy traffic and a documented escalation of domestic abuse, the staff see some very disturbing cases.

Ruth designed her program while keeping all of these situations in mind.

> It was a packed house. It turned out that many of the orderlies showed up as well, which threw me off a bit since I couldn't really turn anyone away.

She planned to present the program in one day and for two groups, running from 7 A.M. to 7 P.M. They arrived in two shifts, so that their stations were always manned. In effect, Ruth had to give the same program twice in one day.

Ruth will offer comments throughout the text, for this is the material she used to help her get started. She will help you understand some of my theories and catch-phrases and will add some experienced wisdom of her own. Watch for her notes throughout the book.

Adults Are
Always Learning

Adults will learn no matter what. Learning is as natural as rest or play. With or without workbooks, visual aids, inspiring trainers or classrooms, adults will manage to learn. Course facilitators can, however, make a difference in what people learn, and in how well they learn it.

If adults know why they are learning, and if the reason fits their needs as they perceive them, they will learn quickly and deeply.

—Malcolm Knowles, 1984

Information is readily available to anyone who can read, see, or hear. As adults, we choose to focus our attention on the information we consider valuable. We also tend to avoid or overlook information that initially seems difficult, boring, lengthy, or insignificant. The filters in our heads—the ones that decide for us what's important and what's not—are in constant operation.

Therefore, designers and presenters of material for adult learners have a challenge before them. Selecting the right information and communicating it in ways that will interest all types of adults might sound daunting, but there are some specific concepts and guidelines that can direct the process. While they will not guarantee success, these guides will at least ensure that the audience will be involved and interested.

As I began developing my stress workshop, I was encouraged by knowing that adults will always learn. My job was to help them learn efficiently.

Characteristics of the Adult Learner

By definition, adults are people who have taken responsibility for their own lives. Adults need to be treated as capable individuals who are in charge of themselves and their actions. Anyone developing a program for and teaching adults must initially consider several important points.

Adults are independent.

Adults need to have their independence and self-sufficiency acknowledged. They resent being taught like children. You need to engage adults in the learning process through active participation and self-direction. Self-direction allows participants to evaluate the importance of different subjects for themselves and then choose the areas they would like to focus on.

Adults are experienced.

Adults are a rich resource for one another and for the facilitator of any program. They bring a great deal of experience and knowledge with them. This is true for all adults, no matter what their education or skill level may be. Life experiences are the foundation for new learning.

> Sometimes I felt like the participants were teaching the session all by themselves, they had so many examples and anecdotes. So I let them roll with it for a while. Hospital staffing situations, especially stressful ones, lend themselves towards long, involved stories, so I had to keep a handle on some of the more proficient yarn spinners!

Adults are goal-oriented.

Adults are ready to learn when the opportunity presents itself. The trick is not to wait around for the opportunity. Many situations can trigger the need or desire to learn. For example: a new job or task, losing a job, or change of any kind.

The drive to learn can be induced in adults if they can be made to recognize a goal that they want to achieve or to perceive a gap between where they are now and where they want or need to be.

Adults are sensitive.

Adults take errors personally and are more likely than children to let them affect their self-esteem. Thus, adults tend to use tried and true solutions and often are unwilling to take risks. Trainers should, therefore, design calculated risks that will be challenging but that will allow most participants to feel secure.

Adults are practical.

Educational materials for adults must be directly related to life situations and must incorporate relevant tasks, problems, or situations. For example, a program for college students titled "Instructional Design" would be better titled "Designing Course Materials For On-The-Job-Training" for employees of an organization. Participants need to know at the onset of the program how it will relate to a current or future need in their work life.

The nurses and orderlies had been complaining for months about the pressure they were under so I knew they would be interested in stress management. My challenge was to persuade them that the workshop would really be helpful.

Adults are motivated by many rewards.

Programs and workshops that emphasize increased self-esteem, greater self-confidence, and recognition of individuality achieve a better response from participants than those that stress better jobs and salaries.

Are you like me? Do you just have millions of questions already? What materials should I choose? How shall I present the information? Where do I start? How do I start? Who is my audience? What do they need to know? How long should this take? What questions will people have? What do these people already know?

Don't worry. This book explains it all. My sessions went pretty well, and I'll be here to guide you through.

What is Your Style of Learning?

Adult learners bring their past learning experiences into any new learning situation. Some adults sat passively as children in their grade school classes and were lectured to, quizzed, and then graded. This worked perfectly for them. Others enjoyed competing in school, working in teams, or discussing new information among peers in order to synthesize, digest, and learn. If these styles worked for them in the past, most adult learners will typically rely upon them in any learning situation. There are four basic learning styles that encompass most adult learners; you will find, however, that many people fit into more than one category.

Perceivers

Their learning style is concrete and experienced-based. Perceivers interpret things in light of their experiences. They need to be involved in what they learn, and they enjoy discussions and simulations. They are people-oriented and base their judgments on sensations. They can be described as understanding, receptive, practical, insightful, and concrete.

Observers

Their learning style is passive and externally based. Observers learn by watching demonstrations, examples, and films and by listening to lectures. They are information-oriented and base their judgments on the knowledge they have absorbed from available sources. They can be described as impartial, watchful, reflective, guarded, and reserved.

I think I'm an observer, but I've learned that others aren't, so instead of saying "Here's how you should do it," I try to say, "Well, here's the way I learned to do it. Why don't you give it a try?"

Feelers

Their learning style is characterized by a hands-on orientation to learning. Feelers need to be involved in activities, projects, games, role plays, case studies, and small group discussions. They are "action oriented" and base their judgments on the results of their first hand experiences. They are best described as being involved, aggressive, daring, tactile, active, and "future oriented."

This describes a lot of my nursing staff, especially Amy. I never have to search for what she's thinking. In fact, she was so helpful in our session, in terms of examples and explanations, that I decided to train her so she could train others.

Thinkers

Their learning style is abstract and analytical. Thinkers need to be involved in problem-solving, analysis, and logical discussions. They benefit from presentation of theories to support data. They are oriented towards the logical and the symbolic, and base their judgments, which tend to be straight forward, on analysis. They are best described as being evaluative, logical, abstract, theoretical, pragmatic, and rational.

Adam is definitely a thinker. He won't listen to any advice or tips, only hard data. I had some trouble getting Adam to adapt to his position when I promoted him to the head nursing job. He always waits to see results in the form of hard data before judging his own performance; however, accurate, reliable data is often hard to find.

In any group you're likely to find people with each of these learning styles. That's why it's important to present your material in a variety of ways that will engage everyone in the class.

The relevance of this information is twofold:

1. Before training

As a designer and developer of adult learning materials, it is important to include something for everyone in the program material. For example:

- a simulation experience for the perceiver
- a demonstration or lecture for the observer
- a case study for the feeler
- a statistical analysis or other data which supports your objectives for the thinker

2. During training

As the facilitator, it is important to recognize each participant's style of learning. Once you've done this, you'll be able to relate the material to each person and maximize his or her experience.

If you work with people long enough, you'll understand their learning styles. Of course, if you have over sixty students in the course of two programs, you'll find it difficult to tune into each one individually. In that case, you'll tailor your presentation in terms of groups rather than individuals. For instance, I addressed all the orderlies with the understanding that their medical knowledge is not equal to that of the nurses. I asked them how this course applied to their work.

What is Your Style of Learning?

Recognizing your own learning style will help you assess the styles of your participants. With this knowledge you'll find that you are better able to personalize your program design, and you'll have a pattern which you can confidently follow when delivering your program.

Circle the letter of the phrase that best fits you.

1. Other people would describe me as:

    a. a reflective and complex person.

    b. people oriented and able to get the job done.

    c. analytical and logical.

    d. responsible and involved in what I do.

2. When I communicate with others, I:

    a. concentrate on solving current problems and issues.

    b. get impatient with people who have not done their homework.

    c. start to fidget and lose interest if other people go into too much detail.

    d. listen to all the relevant details and then take some time to reflect before I respond.

3. The first thing I like to do when I prepare for a program is:

    a. identify the specific goal of the presentation and prepare an outline containing facts which support my objectives.

    b. consider different approaches to the project and choose the one which best fits my needs.

    c. research supporting information, then use it to create an organized outline.

    d. seek out experienced people for advice, information, and feedback.

4. I would describe myself as:

a. an active doer, a risk taker, an involved participant, a questioner.

b. a receptive learner; practical, yet feeling; a people person; needing involvement.

c. a careful observer, impartial, reflective, sometimes tentative.

d. analytical, logical, a rational pragmatist, theoretical.

5. When I work on a project, I:

a. seek to advance my knowledge in that area or subject.

b. want the work to be stimulating and exciting and involve me in discussions with others.

c. concentrate mainly on the approach, making sure it is systematic and can be logically carried out.

d. need to be sure the work is important enough to justify the time and energy I will spend on it.

6. When I learn something new, I:

a. need to see specific examples of the new tasks or skills and discuss my progress with others.

b. require a structured learning approach directed by an expert who can explain the theory behind the new material.

c. prefer to do hands-on projects complemented by group discussion.

d. like to have someone explain the new tasks or skills to me, then show me how to do them.

7. When I come across people who do not agree with me, I:

a. stay calm and explain my point of view simply and logically.

b. explain the reasoning behind my ideas and try to persuade them to take my view.

c. listen to their ideas and reconsider my own point of view.

d. encourage them to discuss all the different ideas and work towards a compromise, if necessary.

8. When I am given a rush assignment by my boss, I:

   a. calmly adjust my schedule to accommodate the extra work and begin the project immediately.

   b. look through my files to see if I have any useful information from former projects, then gather as much resource material as I can before beginning.

   c. discuss the assignment with my peers and use their suggestions as a starting point, then consider whether any former assignments or projects would be useful to me.

   d. write down a few ideas, talk to one or two people to determine the best one, then go ahead with my outline.

9. When I think about a problem at work, I usually:

   a. consider the causes of the problem and concentrate on resolving them.

   b. focus on solutions to the present situation.

   c. look at the big picture, or the overall context of the problem.

   d. try to pinpoint my feelings about the situation and remain open to various solutions.

10. The career(s) I feel I am well suited for include (select one or more):

   a. planner, researcher.

   b. accountant, engineer.

   c. trainer, marketing, sales.

   d. production, management.

Analyzing Your Style

As we know, we are all different. Our reactions to certain problems and situations are unique. This assessment provides you with a rough summary of your "orientation," or the way you learn, think, communicate, and solve problems. It also provides insight into other people's orientation in these areas. This information is crucial to the process of training adults.

Consider, for example, trying to appeal to a thinker. You can't say things like, "Put yourself in someone else's shoes," or "Share how that makes you feel." You've got to give the thinker some facts, give the observer some distance, give the perceiver some symbols, and so on. Knowing your orientation and that of your students will help you present your information in the most effective manner.

For each number below, check the letter which matches the response you chose for that corresponding number on the previous worksheet. The column with the highest total indicates your learning style.

	Observer	Feeler	Thinker	Perceiver
1.	a. ___	d. ___	c. ___	b. ___
2.	d. ___	c. ___	b. ___	a. ___
3.	c. ___	d. ___	a. ___	b. ___
4.	c. ___	a. ___	d. ___	b. ___
5.	a. ___	b. ___	c. ___	d. ___
6.	d. ___	c. ___	b. ___	a. ___
7.	b. ___	d. ___	a. ___	c. ___
8.	b. ___	d. ___	a. ___	c. ___
9.	c. ___	d. ___	a. ___	b. ___
10.	a. ___	c. ___	b. ___	d. ___
Totals	___	___	___	___

Learning Conditions

One of the main goals for you, as a facilitator of the learning process for adults, is to establish a positive climate in which the educational experience can enhance performance on the job. The following observations describe some environmental aspects of adult learning and pinpoint conditions that will maximize the learning experience.

1. Adults have a lot to lose when they enter a group educational experience (self-identity, self-esteem, status, and peer-group respect).

> You have to put some safeguards in place that will promote group respect and interpersonal knowledge. I started by helping everyone become comfortable with the orderlies' unannounced attendance and by making sure that people understood each other's perspective on stress. To accomplish this, I asked each nurse and orderly to stand, say his or her name, and briefly state why he or she felt the need to relieve and manage stress. Each person talked for about half a minute, so it took about fifteen minutes.

2. Most adults, at one time or another, experience doubts about their adequacy and have fears about falling behind or being replaced.

> Here's where things got dicey. Each time I offered some praise or respect in response to something said by a regular nurse, Adam, who is a head nurse, got nervous and questioned the nurse's authority. It was clear that Adam still wasn't too confident about his position. When I suggested that he relax, he got defensive.

3. Many adults have developed a reflex resistance toward authority.

> I didn't sense a great deal of resistance, except for the run-ins one often has, especially when relating to or delegating to employees older than you. Many of my nurses have more experience than me and resent any implication that I might know more than they do.

4. Adults have well-established emotional frameworks consisting of values, attitudes, and tendencies that must be recognized as well as appreciated.

5. Learning experiences produce pressure for change and create anxiety and disorientation for a time.

> In your guidelines, you need to provide safety, mutual commitment, respect, and choices. I made sure each member was allowed to ask questions and to dissent. Each member needs to feel that they're contributing and filtering at the same time—a tall order. Respect for experience is a must; get to know who you are talking to before you make a conclusion about his or her personality.

6. All individuals distort communication by selectively filtering information.

> Speaking of filtering . . . most of the nurses know that I used to be a nurse but haven't been directly in contact with patients for several years. So their filters are saying, this lady doesn't REALLY know what she's talking about. Well, the truth is, I do, but their filters are on full blast anyway. You will gain credibility as you continue to demonstrate your knowledge.

Summary

Knowing the capabilities, limitations, needs, and desires of your audience will help you create an effective program. When you apply what you know about how and why adults learn, you create the best possible learning environment. Personalizing this knowledge, with respect to each individual in your group, is not a "finishing touch." It is essential to the success of your program.

Learning is a personal experience, different in many ways for each learner. Designing a program and organizing material so that each individual will obtain maximum benefit can be an arduous process. It may require a lot of starts and stops, hours of frustration and confusion. Yet, considering the best ways to create a positive environment and adding those final touches to your program may be the most rewarding aspects of the process.

> *None but the humble become good teachers of adults. In an adult class the students' experience counts as much as the teacher's knowledge.*
>
> —Edward Lindeman

Seeing my participants enjoy and learn from my program was truly fulfilling. I have one last thought to share with you before you start designing your program. What can you do if one or several members of your group are just plain reluctant to learn? As a facilitator you have an obligation to make every participant as comfortable as possible. However, dealing with each one separately is a waste of the group's time. If their behavior is truly disruptive, a brief acknowledgment of their concerns may encourage them to participate; whereas singling them out and embarrassing will not be helpful. If those participants will be part of other groups you lead, consider enlisting their cooperation and assistance prior to the session. Model the behavior you wish to see in your participants and deal with any difficult group members before or after your session, if necessary.

Now on to your first action plan! Get those pencils out and we will provide the paper!

Your Notes/Action Plan

This section will help you to start applying what you've learned. As you answer these questions, think about some long and short term goals you have now but didn't have before you picked up this book.

Set yourself up for success by choosing attainable goals. Start with small steps in familiar areas and eventually move toward the unfamiliar. Move slowly and let yourself gain understanding as you go along. Know where you started from and give yourself credit for your progress. This process ensures that you become better at things you already do well and familiar with new concepts.

I have found that I am already proficient at addressing these adult learning issues:

1. _____

2. _____

3. _____

I have learned that these adult learning issues exist and deserve my attention:

1. _____

2. _____

3. _____

My short-term goals for the above items are as follows:

1. _____

2. _____

3. _____

My long-term goals for the above items are as follows:

1. _____

2. _____

3. _____

Ruth's Notes/Action Plan

Here's the way I filled this out. Remember to keep a copy of your action plan with you and update it often. You'll be surprised how often your specific goals change into more challenging tasks.

I have found that I am already proficient at addressing these adult learning issues:

1. Seeing who needs more help and who doesn't.

2. Knowing how much to say the first time around.

3. Watching my nursing team for mistakes and costly, stressful shortcuts.

I have learned that these adult learning issues exist and deserve my attention:

1. Using observational skills to enhance listening abilities makes communication easier.

2. Observation is only one mode of facilitating and does not work in every situation.

3. Examples and anecdotes reinforce concepts and maintain interest.

My short-term goals for the above items are as follows:

1. Make a short list of real examples.

2. Prepare a role-play to help the audience visualize the differences between immediate care-related stress and compounding, additive stressors.

3. Listen for the outsiders' (orderlies) opinions because they often have a useful perspective.

My long-term goals for the above items are as follows:

1. Foster better communication with the members of my team who don't always see eye-to-eye.

2. Insert my own opinions more often (because they actually respect my supervision)!

3. Keep upgrading my EXAMPLES list.

Design
Development

Design is, among other things, the process by which your brain makes itself visible. Your program design is all your own—your world of known facts, shaped by your creative elements, and drawn within the limits of those little things we call goals, which unfortunately, are not all your own.

Goals belong to your participants, too. They have, as we already explained, their own set of goals, the attainment of which you have been asked to facilitate.

Design lies at the heart of every program or workshop that has change as an objective—whether it is a change in behavior or a change in information, training, or skills. Design is a plan of sequential steps which lead to the achievement of a certain goal or set of objectives. Design is, at its foundation, a plan to challenge the creativity and imagination of both the designer and the participants.

My objective was to change participants' behaviors (their reactions to stress) and their use of coping mechanisms (fostering a continued healthy reaction to stress).

Design development is an ambiguous term that can mean almost anything. Have you ever developed an egg? You can—ask any chef. For our purposes, though, development is the process by which you, after considering and outlining a program, mold and shape it into a consistent, applicable, and entertaining whole. So when we say development, think molding, shaping, contouring, and making unique.

The process of designing and developing an effective program for adult learners requires more than merely throwing information out to your audience. Without determining what you specifically want your learners to take away with them, you will achieve neither your goals nor theirs. You'll be wasting everyone's time and effort.

Performance goals will help you focus sharply and aim directly. By combining your knowledge of who your learners are and how you expect them to progress, you can specifically guide your participants toward successful outcomes. This chapter will help you define those goals.

A detailed outline and guide are essential to developing an effective program. They provide you with a plan that organizes your material and supports your role as facilitator. By mastering your material and the structure of your program, you'll develop the confidence and freedom to experiment and to be creative.

This chapter contains "**How-tos**" for putting information into an effective content plan. There is an exercise to help you think specifically about participant needs and wants and an explanation of how to convert this information into learning goals.

We have included general concepts of **outlining** to show you how to identify your major points and organize your material into a comprehensive facilitator's guide. Previously formulated pages are incorporated into the resource material for you to use in each section.

We then offer a complete description of **five useful techniques** to consider in the development of your program. Definitions, examples, and hints concerning these techniques serve as a reference guide for designing all programs. We also present some ways to create tests that will help both you and the learners assess progress and program effectiveness.

Program design

Remember, "design" encompasses the concepts of challenge, creativity, imagination, and the act of planning. An effective program incorporates a balance of these four elements.

Your satisfaction comes when you start to see the results of your own creativity.

4

Determining Goals and Expectations

A participant analysis will help you make some basic decisions about where to start the program, what materials to use, what examples and exercises would be appropriate, what rewards or interests would help motivate your group, and what group members need to know, think, feel, or be able to do when they leave this program. Most important, a participant analysis will help you determine your own goals—what should the objectives of this program be, and how will you, the designer, determine if you have been successful?

At this point, you are ready to create a profile of your audience. You have already thought about your participants' learning styles, but they're not only a bunch of thinkers and feelers; they have some very specific goals and expectations. You need to analyze and address those expectations at the beginning as you begin your program design.

> Although your class expects you to start at step D, teaching the class, be sure that you start at Step A, participant analysis. I've always been sorry when I neglected that step.

Describing participants

On the worksheet that follows, write your response to the questions. This is part of your participant analysis. Jot down any questions you need to ask as well. Feel free to write on the worksheet. A copy of it, and of all the worksheets, is included in the Resource section of this book. You can photocopy and use them as you prepare for other classes.

> Use my notes as a guide. How did I answer the questions? Take a look . . . And keep this group profile handy. You will need it to write goals and complete your facilitator's guide. Remember, you don't have to be too specific.

What information do they need from you?

My staff members needed to know how to change their daily habits and attitudes so that the stress of the health-care workplace could be better managed.

What rewards will be important to them for coming and listening to you? Do they come to the program willingly or because they have to?

Basically they all knew they had to come, not because I formally required it, but because they needed the information. THAT NEED is the best advertisement you can ask for.

What background and skills do they bring to the program (education, job knowledge, interpersonal skills, etc.)?

Out of 70 people total, I've got 55 registered nurses, some part-time, some full-time, some with 20 years of experience, some registered last year. Then I've got some interns enrolled at the midwifery program across town who train here for their clinical test. I've got a group of orderlies and desk clerks who really get in the thick of the battle in the ER, especially on a hot Fourth of July. These participants range in age from 16 to 60. Their experience ranges from 3 weeks to 25 years.

▪▬▬▬▷ Describing Participants

What information do they need from me?

_____

_____

_____

_____

_____

What rewards for coming will be important to them?

_____

_____

_____

_____

_____

What background skills do they bring to the program?

_____

_____

_____

_____

_____

Questions I need to ask to help me better understand these participants:

_____

_____

_____

_____

_____

▰▰▰▰▷ Describing Participants' Learning Goals

Review your notes on the previous worksheet and any other information about your future participants that you may need to include. In this section, you will further specify your participants' learning goals.

Now fill out the following worksheet as specifically as you can. The more thoroughly you can describe what your participants need and want to know, the more accurate your program goals will be. Also, consider management requests and your own expertise as you decide what to include in your program.

> I suggest you get another piece of paper here. And you may not even use this profile as much as we're telling you to. Sometimes just writing down as much information as you possibly can—as long as it's all about your participants—is helpful enough to let you begin designing.

1. What do you feel that your participants really need to know? (These are their learning goals and will eventually be molded into your performance goals.)

   _____

   _____

   _____

2. Does management have any additional goals that need to be included and are not covered above?

   _____

   _____

   _____

3. What do you believe is important for your participants to learn?

   _____

   _____

   _____

4. If these goals conflict, which are most important? Can they all be reached to some extent?

_____

_____

_____

What Are You Learning?

Learning can be described in three categories or domains:

- **Cognitive:** dealing with knowledge, comprehension, application, analysis, synthesis, and evaluation.
- **Affective:** dealing with feelings, attitudes, and values.
- **Psychomotor:** dealing with actions, movement, and muscle coordination.

It's important to carefully consider the domain of learning where you expect the most change from your participants. If your teaching relates mostly to the cognitive domain, don't be surprised if you don't see much change in participants' attitudes and actions. If you want to resolve conflict in your workplace, you must address feelings, not talk about brain chemistry. If mechanical errors are under consideration, specific procedures must be taught. A pep talk on being careful will be far less helpful.

> Although most instruction is in the cognitive domain (thinking, remembering, etc.—typical classroom activities), other parts of instruction may be directed towards changing feelings and attitudes. It turns out that, even though I thought I'd be instructing primarily on emotional (affective) issues, much of my teaching had to do with specialized, cognitive responses. I had to teach people specific ways in which they could think about stressful situations and respond effectively.

Once you have established your learning goals, you can transform them into performance goals, which are learning objectives tailored to your expectations of the participants' progress.

6

Describing Outcomes

A performance goal or objective is the description of a measurable outcome. Performance goals state the intentions of the program. Begin by describing the desired end product or result you want to achieve. What will the participants have in the way of new skills, knowledge, or behavior by the time they complete your program? These goals become the criteria by which you select materials, outline content, develop instructional procedures, and prepare tests.

Without performance goals, programs lack substance and focus merely on delivery and means. They are not the foundation of your program; they are the walls that rest on the foundation of the learners' goals. They will determine how high your building goes (in other words, how extensive the design of your program need be).

Components of performance goals

In order for your program goals to be effective, they must communicate specific requirements. Here are some characteristics to be used as guides—it will not always be necessary to include every statement.

To write a performance goal, you must include:

1. **A "what" statement**
   Identify the behavior or performance by a name; specify the kind of performance that will be accepted as evidence that the learner has achieved the goal.

2. **A "when" statement**
   Describe the conditions under which the behavior will be expected to occur.

3. **A "how well" statement**
   Specify the criteria of acceptable performance by describing how well the learner must perform in order to be considered acceptable.

Keep in mind that while constructing test items you must first think about goals that you will need to test to ensure that you stay on target. This helps me a lot.

Writing performance goals

True performance goals focus on the importance of what the learner must do, know, feel, etc. Make your intentions clear by thinking of the learner:

1. Be brief and to the point.

2. Include only one major item in each goal.

3. Use action words to describe the expected results.

4. Specify results in measurable terms wherever it's appropriate.

5. Check to see if you have covered all the important issues.

Words that are open to
many interpretations:

- know
- understand
- appreciate
- enjoy
- believe
- experience

Words that are open to
fewer interpretations:

- identify
- solve
- list
- compare
- translate
- write

Here's a brief list of the performance goals I developed for my training session. I could begin to meet my criteria for success if employees understood information, felt better, and took certain actions, but only the assessment described in item three would truly judge whether participants had reached the goals.

1. After attending class, staff members will be able to identify and use at least five stress-reducing tips, stress-managing attitudes, and stress-relieving exercises both on the job and at home.

2. Employees will develop and use a set of evaluative procedures to keep each other on their toes, stress-management-wise. This will probably include a daily group-therapy type meeting, before each shift change to let all nurses air gripes, talk about the day, etc.

3. At their next employee evaluation period, employees will show a 20 percent increase in overall points. Most of this improvement will be the effect of better stress-management scores.

Now use the worksheet on the next page to define performance goals for your training session.

✏️➤ Performance Goals for Session: _____

After the session is complete:

Learners will know:

_____

_____

Attainment of this goal will be measured by:

_____

_____

Learners will feel:

_____

_____

Attainment of this goal will be measured by:

_____

_____

_____

Learners will do:

_____

_____

_____

Attainment of this goal will be measured by:

_____

_____

_____

Preparing a Program Outline

A program outline is an organized, logical arrangement of the content and flow of your program. This outline covers all the key points expressed in your goals. In other words, this is a plan which will make the goals happen.

The information in your outline must be useful and transferable to your participants. Remember to include all the important aspects of your program that you expect your participants to retain. For this reason, a good program outline usually consists of the titles and subtitles of your intended program.

The outline form we have included in this lesson is one of many possible forms. It is just the beginning of the process of planning and writing a teaching guide.

Some important rules to remember

1. Separate complex ideas into several simpler ideas; these will probably be subtitles.
2. Present information in a logical sequence.
3. Go from general to specific (for instance "overview, details, summary").
4. Contextualize information so it makes sense to your participants.
5. Focus on one important idea at a time.

There are many ways of putting these components on paper. This format is certainly not the only acceptable one, nor may it be the best one for your purposes. However, it does include all the elements we feel are necessary for a successful outline.

Your program outline

This exercise will form the basis for your teaching plan, which is discussed in the following lesson. Be specific with this outline, but remember, it is an outline, not a complete script.

Review your performance goals. These will be your TITLES. Then write down the main points that support your goals. For our purposes, stick to five or fewer per title.

The number of goals you choose will depend on the amount of information you have to present and the amount of time you have to work with.

If you have been told to cover your topic in 2 to 3 hours, the key points you choose to cover will have to fit comfortably within this time frame. If you have a whole day to cover your topic, you can go into more detail or add more key points. Compare the information you want to cover and the time you need to do it adequately—do they match? My outline appears on the next page. I believe it will be helpful to you when you develop your own.

After you read through Ruth's program outline, complete your own on the page following Ruth's. If you prefer another format, feel free to use that, but be sure to prepare this outline in some form before moving to the next section on developing teaching plans.

Ruth's Program Outline

Program Name: Stress-Management for Health Care Professionals

Introductions

Allow about twenty minutes for individual introductions; this should put most people at ease. Make sure everyone is listening! Introduce the program concepts and goals; introduce role plays as a way to accomplish those goals; break some ice.

Goal 1

Staff members will be able to identify and use at least five stress-reducing tips, stress-managing attitudes, and stress-relieving exercises both on the job and at home.

First role play: at least seven people, playing roles of administrator, ER tech, patient, patient's mother, ER attendee, and waiting surgeon. The main stressed-out employees in this group should be the ER tech and the ER attendee. They're the ones answering all the questions, placating everyone, and keeping the surgeons off their backs.

Second role play: administrative stressors. Attendee and head nurse battling for position on a new research project, while administration wants neither of them. The most stressed-out individual is the administrative person.

Separate into three groups of about twelve, each group facilitated by a head nurse. Discuss reactions to role plays and possible stress-relief and stress-management plans. Regroup and discuss further. After discussion review, on chalkboard or white board write the most popular stress-relief modes.

Goal 2

Employees will develop and use a set of evaluative procedures that will probably include a daily group-therapy type meeting before each shift change.

Assess all employees' progress by placing all employees who *didn't* act in role plays, into role plays of their own. Each person should be able, in smaller groups, to demonstrate newly learned on-site stress-management techniques. These techniques should include at least one, but not all, of the following: pre-shift exercises, stretches and attitude adjustments; on-shift attitude adjustment techniques; post-shift debriefing.

Goal 3

At their next employee evaluation period, employees will show a 20 percent increase in overall points.

Develop, with employees, a list of both tangible and intangible goals, i.e. employee evaluation scores and fewer tangible stress-management reactions.

Program Outline

Session: _____

Performance goal _____

1. _____
2. _____
3. _____
4. _____
5. _____

Performance goal _____

1. _____
2. _____
3. _____
4. _____
5. _____

Performance goal _____

1. _____
2. _____
3. _____
4. _____
5. _____

Teaching Plans

Teachers aren't really teachers without teaching plans. In fact, without teaching plans, they're lecturers, orators, or professional speakers. A teacher is called a teacher because he or she has specific performance goals, which are congruent with the students' learning goals and are articulated in an outline and plan which will bring these goals into fruition.

A written teaching plan forces you to organize your material. It is important to remember that each point must make sense by itself and that the points must be presented in logical sequence.

> The written plan was a valuable aid throughout my program. It compelled me to ask myself the following questions:
>
> - Do I have all the materials I need?
>
> - Have I covered every point?
>
> - Am I spending too much time in one area?

Preparing your teaching plan

Following this page are some basic teaching plan formats with explanations and instructions on each page. Many of the pages also contain notes that Ruth made as she developed her teaching plans. You'll also find several complete pages from Ruth's plan.

This process will be most effective if you focus on a specific program, either one you are planning or one that you might present in the future. There is a clean set of forms included at the end of the Resource section for you to copy and use for your next program. A detailed discussion of techniques for program designers follows this exercise.

The forms appear as follows:

1. Preparation

2. Participant List

3. Materials List

4. Program Cover Page

5. Program Objectives

6. Program Description

7. Program Content Outline

8. Agenda Notes

9. Facilitator's Guide: Introduction Notes

10. Facilitator's Guide: Program Notes

11. Facilitator's Guide: Visual Notes

12. Facilitator's Guide: Worksheet

13. Facilitator's Guide: Conclusion Notes

Let's go. This is where your creativity really shows through. You can use the following forms as both practice worksheets and final teaching plans. When you facilitate a similar program, the majority of the work will be done!

You'll see that sometimes I followed the worksheets exactly; other times I didn't. Do whatever works for you, but please fill them out. The book will be much more helpful if you do.

✏️ 1. Preparation

Questions and points to consider

1. Is there anything participants need to bring to your program?
2. Is advance preparation necessary for participants?
3. If participants need to bring supplies or complete pre-work, send them an announcement letter ten days to two weeks in advance.
4. Make sure directions are clear, and include a phone number the participants can call if they have questions.
5. Include the time, place, and date of the program, as well as any other essential instructions.

Information for your announcement

Welcome to (workshop title) _____

It will be held on (date) _____

from (starting and ending times) _____

The workshop location is (address/building/room, as needed) _____

_____

Directions to location (if needed) _____

_____

Prior to the session, please prepare by (reading, listing, etc.) _____

_____

Bring to the session (workbook, notepad, etc.) _____

_____

For more information, contact _____

at (phone #) _____

✏️ 2. Participant List

If at all possible, obtain a list of participants. Think about the kind of information you need to personalize your program and ask for it. If you will be offering other programs for the same groups, you may want to develop a paper or card file with a record for each participant or enter information in a computer database program.

Use the following outline, adding any information that will be important for you. Consider updating the file after the program is complete, particularly if you expect to see the participants again. Be sure to record the programs each person has attended.

Name: _____

Telephone number: _____

Company: _____

Job title: _____

Department: _____

Other information: _____

_____

_____

Program 1 / date: _____

Program 2 / date: _____

Program 3 / date: _____

Notes: _____

_____

I left lots of room for notes so I could be better prepared the next time I taught the same people.

✎⟹ 3. Materials List

This list will let you organize the material you actually use during your program. Fill it out now, but come back to it after you have read the Resource Guide at the end of this chapter.

Program name: _____

Leader's resources: _____

_____

Teaching materials: slides, overheads, computer software, files, and handouts (name/ number of copies) _____

_____

_____

_____

Equipment: easel/paper/markers, white board/markers, overhead projector, slide projector, screen, computer, etc. _____

_____

_____

My main resource was "Stress Management in the Workplace"; it has many charts and step-by-step techniques for groups.

Make 15 copies of all handouts (my copies are in color so I can find the notes I scribble all the time.)

Equipment is already in place. Handouts will be distributed individually at each session.

I feel much more confident after I check off every item on my materials list.

4. Program Cover Page

Prepare a cover sheet for the set of materials you bring to the session with you. You may want to copy the page and distribute it during the session. Participants can then file it with their other handouts. The cover sheet should include:

Program name

Session date

Sponsoring organization or department

Time and duration

My cover sheet was quite simple.

Stress Management for the Health Care Professional

May 20, 1998

Nursing Department

One full day, two five hour sessions

✏️════▷ 5. Program Objectives

While you have already filled out something similar to this in Lesson 3, you may want to restate it here as a double check and reminder.

Program name: _____

By the end of this program, participants will be able to:

1. _____
2. _____
3. _____
4. _____
5. _____

These are my final objectives. You can see that they changed a bit as I worked on the program.

1. Master attitude adjustment, a specific technique for avoiding tantrums and other reactions not conducive to working in a group under stressful situations.

2. Work within groups, before and after shifts, to constructively manage stress.

3. Use and reuse the stress-manager, a white board set up in both men's and women's lounges on which gripes can be aired.

4. Facilitate interpersonal stress-management by holding pre-shift group meetings.

5. Score a 20 percent increase (prorated to 5 percent to top scorers) on stress-management section of next employee evaluation.

✏️ 6. Program Description

You'll probably have to publicize your program in a newsletter or in some other way. How would you concisely describe your workshop to someone who knows nothing about the topic?

_____

_____

_____

Who is it for?

_____

_____

Are there any prerequisites?

_____

_____

Here's how I described my seminar:

A seminar taking place twice on a light weekday, in which I, as director of Human Resources, share several examples, techniques, and handouts all dealing with and reducing stress-related problems.

It's designed for nurses and other health care professionals (attending midwives, orderlies, and ER clerks).

All attending participants must be involved in a highly stressful job at Arlee County Hospital. Janitors, window washers, administration above HR, surgeons, and those with strictly desk-bound jobs are encouraged to form their own stress-management seminar and are not invited to this one.

7. Program Content Outline

Put enough detail in your program outline to enable you to use this information as the foundation of your program. You will use this information to develop your agenda. For each program segment, you need to make decisions about:

- Materials needed to support goals

- Exercises you want to add

- Discussion segments

- Small and large group work

- Individual projects

- Transition spots

- Participant handouts

- Lectures

- Role plays

- Demonstrations

- Audio/visual aids

Here are some of the issues I thought about as I prepared my outline.

- Transitions: This is a five hour course, and I know that most people's attention spans do not exceed 45 minutes. This would allow ample time for four 30-minute role plays, with handouts and white-board lessons as transitions.

- Materials: Covered, except for handouts.

- Exercises: Besides the other role plays, three of the handouts require writing and complex association.

Discussion segments will fill in all remaining time. I have a feeling discussion will be a most beneficial tool, whether in small or large groups. Individual assessments will be evident by the last, small-group role plays, which are led by head nurses.

Program Content Outline

Program title: _____

Segment 1: _____

_____

_____

_____

Segment 2: _____

_____

_____

_____

Segment 3: _____

_____

_____

_____

Segment 4: _____

_____

_____

_____

Segment 5: _____

_____

_____

_____

8. Agenda

The next step is to develop a detailed, minute-by-minute agenda. That can be hard to do the first time, but it gets easier as you gain experience. Although it's hard to estimate how long various segments might take, it's important that you put your schedule in writing. That's the only way you'll know whether you're on track or will need to make adjustments to reach all your goals.

This was my agenda for the stress management seminar.

MORNING	AFTERNOON	
8:00–8:45	(2:00–2:45)	Introductions with coffee, bagels, juice (finger sandwiches, juice, coffee)
9:00–9:30	(3:00–3:30)	First role play: the ER
9:30–9:45	(3:30–3:45)	Small group discussion
9:45–10:00	(3:45–4:00)	Large group discussion with visuals
10:00–10:15	(4:00–4:15)	Exercise 1 with visuals: on the job stress-relievers
10:15–10:30	(4:15–4:30)	Break
10:30–10:45	(4:30–4:45)	Second role play: administration
10:45–11:00	(4:45–5:00)	Small group discussion
11:00–11:15	(5:00–5:15)	Large group discussion with visuals
11:15–11:30	(5:15–5:30)	Exercise 2 with visuals: attitude adjustment and habit forming stressors
11:30–11:45	(5:30–5:45)	Break
11:45–12:00	(5:45–6:00)	Third (small group) role play: on your own
12:00–12:45	(6:00–6:45)	Large group discussion covering all role plays and assessments
12:45–1:00	(6:45–7:00)	Wrap-up with visuals and last handout

Agenda Notes

Program title: _____

Start	End	Segment
_____	_____	_____
_____	_____	_____
_____	_____	_____
_____	_____	_____
_____	_____	_____
_____	_____	_____
_____	_____	_____
_____	_____	_____
_____	_____	_____
_____	_____	_____
_____	_____	_____
_____	_____	_____
_____	_____	_____
_____	_____	_____
_____	_____	_____
_____	_____	_____
_____	_____	_____
_____	_____	_____
_____	_____	_____

9. Facilitator's Guide: Introduction

The Facilitator's Guide is a series of sheets which you'll use for the actual delivery of your presentation. You'll learn more about presentation in Chapter Three.

The introduction page includes your opening statement and presents your approach, i.e. how you plan on setting up the workshop and accomplishing your goals. The way you begin is critical, so take the time to write out the opening statement.

I decided to capture people's interest by mentioning a TV program that many of the nurses and orderlies watch.

How many of you saw "ER" last night? And how many of you agree with me that the real ER is ten times more annoying, stressful, aggravating, bloody, and downright mean than the one on TV? How many of you are stressed out by your jobs? And I don't mean going home with a knot in your back or some chest angina from too much caffeine. I'm talking about lashing out at your best friend just because he asked you how work was going. I'm talking about dropping your coffee on the third rail and actually considering going to retrieve it. Crazy stuff, huh?

We need to manage our stress. We can't just get rid of it. Stress will always be there, like luggage. You can't just drop it. You have to manage its effect on you and your performance here at Arlee County Hospital.

- Review of objectives

- Participant goals and expectations

- Outline for program with scheduled times

- Norms (the way you want people to interact and take responsibility for their learning)

- Housekeeping items (location of bathrooms, coffee, etc.)

✏️➡ Facilitator's Guide: Introduction Notes

Program title: _____

Opening statement: _____

_____

_____

_____

_____

_____

_____

Review of objectives: _____

_____

_____

Participant goals: _____

_____

_____

Outline for program with scheduled times: _____

_____

_____

Norms: _____

_____

_____

Housekeeping items: _____

_____

10. Facilitator's Guide: Program Notes

Program Note pages are divided into three sections across each page:

1. Major points: In this section, your topics will be organized in order of presentation.

2. Training devices: In this section, list the items you need for the topic.

- Chalkboard
- Handout
- Chart
- Overheads

3. Notes: In this section, make notes on the activity.

- List (on chalkboard)
- Distribute (handout)
- Present (overhead transparencies)
- Set up a role play
- Ask, demonstrate, discuss, etc.

I started my program notes up like this:

MAJOR POINTS	TRAINING DEVICES	NOTES
introduction	chalkboard	list goals
job stress	1st role play handout	distribute handout, form groups, do role plays
relationships	2nd role play handout	distribute handout, do role plays, discuss

✏️ Facilitator's Guide: Program Notes

Major points	Training devices	Notes
_____	_____	_____
_____	_____	_____
_____	_____	_____
_____	_____	_____
_____	_____	_____
_____	_____	_____
_____	_____	_____
_____	_____	_____
_____	_____	_____
_____	_____	_____
_____	_____	_____
_____	_____	_____
_____	_____	_____
_____	_____	_____
_____	_____	_____
_____	_____	_____
_____	_____	_____
_____	_____	_____
_____	_____	_____

11. Facilitator's Guide: Visual Notes

This page in your Facilitator's Guide allows you to plan in advance for a presentation, handout, slide show, overhead set, or display. Put the information for each visual on a separate page in addition to mentioning it in your notes. This page will help you gather all the visuals together for preplanning and will give you the material you need to carry along for the presentation. By storing this page with the visual as well as with the program, you will avoid having to rewrite it every time you use the visual in a different program.

Writing out a reminder page for my visual helped me stay on track when I presented the chart to the group. Now I have it ready for the next session, too.

Chart from "Stress Management in the Workplace"

Used in program: Stress Management for Nurses/Segment Two

Chart stored in Segment Two folder

Main points:

- Keep content clear!
- Concise!
- Easy to read!
- Easy to remember!

✏ Facilitator's Guide: Visual Notes

Visual title: _____

Source: _____

Storage location: _____

Used in programs/segments:

_____

_____

_____

_____

_____

_____

_____

Main points to be made with visual:

_____

_____

_____

_____

_____

_____

_____

_____

_____

12. Facilitator's Guide: Worksheet Notes

The Facilitator's Guide should contain a copy of each worksheet handout you pass out to your participants or include it in a materials packet. Attach a copy of this worksheet cover page to each worksheet. On the copy in your guide, write your own notes and special directions if necessary.

Program title: Stress Management for Nurses

Segment: The Stress of Relationships

Worksheet title: New Ways to Cope with the Stress of Relationships

Main points:

1. Feeling stressed out and upset with other people can affect your work performance. (Present an appropriate example here.)

2. It's your choice to become upset or stay calm.

3. You need to develop strategies that will help you deal with difficult people.

Worksheet includes the following questions:

1. First write at least three instances in which you failed to complete a task because you were upset about something someone said or did to you.

2. In hindsight, what do you think you should have done?

3. How do you think you could correct this problem in the future?

✏️ Facilitator's Guide: Worksheet Notes

Program name: _____

Segment: _____

Worksheet title: _____

Main points to be made with this worksheet:

_____

_____

_____

_____

_____

_____

Describe the worksheet:

_____

_____

_____

_____

_____

_____

_____

_____

_____

13. Facilitator's Guide: Conclusion Notes

The conclusion to your program is even more important than the introduction. If this is an educational session, you want people to leave remembering the key points. If you are trying to facilitate behavior change, you want them to leave with a clear plan for change. On this page in your Facilitator's Guide, record your plan for the conclusion of your program and your concluding statement to participants.

Goal for conclusion:

I want to be sure that all the nurses and orderlies can put into practice what they have learned.

Process:

Each head nurse will take the same twelve people for a third role play (may take two role plays to get everyone involved) and assess each person's performance in terms of motivation and use of new techniques.

Concluding statement:

The jobs that nurses and orderlies have are inherently stressful because our patients come in times of real crisis. We can't make those stressors go away; they're part of the job. But when we learn and practice stress management techniques, we can reduce the effects of stress. Today's session has given us all some new ideas. Let's start using them immediately and we'll all be healthier and happier.

✏ Facilitator's Guide: Conclusion Notes

Goal for conclusion:

_____

_____

_____

Process:

_____

_____

_____

Concluding statement:

_____

_____

_____

_____

_____

_____

_____

_____

_____

_____

_____

_____

_____

Molding and Shaping Your Program

Hopefully you've used the preceding pages to begin formulating your teaching plan. You've designed your program with broad strokes, and there are only two steps left: improve the design and add some details.

Your teaching plan will still need some review and updating, mainly because you're not yet finished with this manual. At this point you need to streamline your program and make it interesting and fun. For example:

Give participants things to hold on to. These tend to work well:
- Articles (handouts DO get read)
- Diagrams
- Charts
- Audiotapes
- Programmed instruction

> I copied and blew up a lot of charts from that book. I wasn't sure how many I'd use. But if I sense the crowd isn't too attentive, I planned to pass out some of the charts for them to see up close.
>
> I had to plan ahead because I needed to get permission from the publisher to photocopy the charts. Be sure to give yourself plenty of time for that step.

Use methods which require participants to experiment and see results, such as:
- Case studies
- Demonstrations
- Role play
- Videotapes
- Exercises
- Worksheets

Use methods which require participants to challenge the old versus the new, such as:
- Role plays
- Structured games
- Exercises
- Self-analysis and assessments

Enhance the participants capacity for creativity and facilitate their innovation by using these techniques:
- Brainstorming
- Mental acuity exercises
- Unstructured games
- Group projects

By allowing my participants some time for 15-minute role play segments on their own, they came up with a lot of stressors I hadn't even thought of. Adam found a team of cardiac nurses who had a particularly bad relationship with one of the surgeons, and he was able to provide some recommendations. This early success helped with the rest of the day, morale-wise.

10

A Word About Testing

You are probably wondering if tests are really necessary for the program you are designing. That question can be answered with another—Are you interested in knowing whether your goals have been reached? Your answer will be "yes" if you are concerned with the quality of your facilitation, the success of your participants, and the necessity for your program. Let's look at ways of constructing and making use of tests.

Constructing tests

What do I test on? Box scores? Quilting? Average rainfall below the Tropic of Capricorn?

Actually, just goals. A test is really nothing more than an opportunity for the participants to demonstrate that they are capable of the performance specified by your agreed upon goals. This means that once you have completed the list of performance goals for a given program, the test content has been defined. All that remains is putting the goals into some form of a test.

Formulate these tests by borrowing from the goals that you wrote at the beginning of this chapter. Go back to your Goals Section and, using one or more testing techniques, create a quiz based on your goals.

A smorgasbord of testing techniques

Six types of tests are described on the following pages. Read about them, then choose those that are most appropriate for your situation.

- Performance tests provide people with a chance to actually demonstrate what they have learned. In a classroom situation, however, you may not be able to use this type of test.

- Paper and pencil tests are the most common tools for discovering whether students have mastered the content of a class and are ready to apply it. Six types of tests are described: performance, short essay, multiple choice, true-false, completion, and matching.

Performance Tests

Because most jobs require some observable activity (operating a computer, speaking to the public, etc.), performance tests are frequently used.

The implied question of a performance test is: "Can you perform this job task?" There are, of course, many ways of asking that question, and it is important that you ask it very clearly. Participants must know exactly what you want them to do. Use the same words you used in writing your goals:

- Demonstrate

- Illustrate

- Manipulate

- Operate

- Assemble

When you arrange the environment for performance testing, try to keep it as realistic as possible. The job aids should be located as near as possible to where the employee would find them on the job. Do not "lead them by the hand" by having all the items laid out in their proper places and sequences. Beware of helping the person being tested with comments such as "Watch out!" or "Are you sure?" Even an outstretched hand or a slight gasp can offer a clue to errors. When this happens, you end up taking the test yourself.

It is sometimes a good idea to ask the participants to explain what they are doing as they go through the demonstration. In this way, you are testing (and they are reviewing) both their manual proficiency and their awareness of the reasons behind their actions. By doing this, you will be measuring understanding, instead of memory, and the participants will be all the richer for the experience they gain even as they are being tested.

Short Essays

Essay questions are the most effective ways to determine whether students really understand what was taught. Essay tests, however, are not easy to construct. They require precise language so students understand exactly what is being asked and exactly what kind of information must be included in their answer.

"Explain the benefits of stretching for stress relief" was a good essay question for us. "Explain how to use stretching" was not because it requires a visual to answer the question completely and correctly. People taking the test became frustrated because they had to guess what I meant by the second question. The first question is much better for evoking the desired response.

Essay questions should give students the chance to organize their ideas, express their judgments, and think for themselves. What words should you use? Again, use active verbs and borrow from your goals:

- Classify
- Interpret
- Contrast
- Define
- Summarize
- Review
- Illustrate
- Compare
- Justify
- Describe
- Discuss

Multiple Choice Questions

This is the "best answer" type of question. Begin by writing a statement. Then divide the first portion of the statement from the second.

> One of my questions began with the statement, "Nicotine and caffeine are both considered stress-inducing substances." I divided this into "Nicotine and caffeine are both considered:" and "stress-inducing substances."

Then come up with two or three false alternatives for the second part of the sentence.

> I came up with: "dangerously addictive substances," "substances which mainly lead to obesity," and "substances that will land you in jail." To keep everyone relaxed, I usually add one obviously false alternative.

And finally, arrange the alternatives in a multiple choice format (a, b, c, d).

> 1. Nicotine and caffeine are both considered
>   a. substances which mainly lead to obesity
>   b. dangerously addictive substances
>   c. stress-inducing substances
>   d. substances that will land you in jail

Beware of the "pattern tendency"—the natural inclination to set up a sequence of right answers. You can avoid this pitfall by deliberately allowing so many "a" answers, so many "b" answers, and so forth in advance, writing the questions to conform to this allocation, and then locating them at random in the final draft.

Multiple choice questions are easy to administer and can be self-graded. They can be used to cover lots of material. Good multiple choice questions, however, are time-consuming to prepare. You need to make sure that your false alternatives are plausible.

True-False Questions

True-false questions should be used to test understanding rather than memory. Recognizing correct facts and figures is often all it takes to bring the answers to mind. However, if a statement requires the student to reason before reaching a conclusion, the true-false question may be very appropriate.

To construct true-false questions, start by writing a series of true statements.

"Restress and distress are two of the dangerous types of stress." "Attitude plays a major role in stress-management." "All stress-management techniques require a change in either habits or attitude."

To make false statements, don't add negative words such as "not" and "never." These and other words such as "almost," "nearly," or "most" should be avoided whenever possible in true-false questions. Such words either hint at the correct answer or make the statements partially true.

The best true-false item has only one alternative and is worded positively:

Here's how I made those statements false: "Restress and Eustress are two of the dangerous types of stress." "Aspirin plays a major role in stress-management." "All stress-management techniques require a change in either habits or vitamin selection."

Obviously, during the preparation of a true-false type test, the questions to be made false should be selected at random so participants will not recognize a pattern that could assist them in guessing the answer.

Completion Questions

These are better for testing memorized information than the true-false questions, because they require the participants to remember information before they write. The question does not provide the answer. They may also be effective in exercising a person's intellect because they require people to recall facts, examine a problem, and write a response.

You can construct a completion question in much the same way as a true-false question. Write a statement you are sure everyone can easily understand. Then decide which words are truly the key words for the information you seek from your participants.

> In this question: "An important physical stress-reliever, best applied before your shift, is the stretching of your back and neck muscles," the key word(s) here are "back" and "neck." So I left them out in the written test.

Another form of completion question escapes the "blank inside a sentence" format by asking the participant to make a list. For example:

> List three ways to quickly reduce physical stress on the job.
> List two ways to facilitate a better argument between you and your colleague.

Generally, the completion question will do a better job of testing than will the true-false question. The person must recall the key words instead of being provided with them. However, true-false questions are generally easier to construct and can be checked more quickly.

Matching Questions

To develop a matching test, write several statements with a similar sentence structure; divide them in a similar place grammatically in each sentence, forming two lists, then reorganize one of the lists. Students must find the appropriate ending to the beginning of each sentence. Students can draw lines between the beginning and ending of each statement.

The ACB model refers to   relaxation

The stress associated with euphoria is   change

Most people in time-crunched situations have   eustress

Guided imagery can be used to facilitate   distress

However, the test will be much easier to score if you place a blank line and number next to the first half of each sentence and place a letter next to the second half.

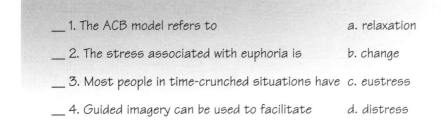

___ 1. The ACB model refers to   a. relaxation

___ 2. The stress associated with euphoria is   b. change

___ 3. Most people in time-crunched situations have c. eustress

___ 4. Guided imagery can be used to facilitate   d. distress

Be sure that the statements are grammatically similar. If the right column contains nouns, verbs, adjectives, and phrases, the structure alone gives clues to the answers.

Directions

The directions which introduce any paper and pencil test should be perfectly clear. Participants must know exactly what you want them to do with a question, so they all have the same opportunity to answer it correctly.

For example, if you have prepared a multiple choice test, specify whether all questions have only one correct answer or whether some questions might have no or several correct answers.

Responses should be made as meaningful as possible. To reinforce what has been learned, whenever possible, instruct participants to write out their responses rather than circle a letter or number.

If it's possible to interpret a question in a way that suggests an answer other than the one you want, someone will make that interpretation. If your directions allow any loopholes, someone will find them. Make your directions clear and specific and ask someone to review the directions and the test.

Before I copied all my testing handouts, I ran them by my husband, who helped me word the directions better. Instead of "Indicate the correct answer with a circle," he suggested something more specific: "Circle the letter which corresponds to the correct answer." He also changed "Fill in the blanks" to "Write out the answer you believe best completes the sentence."

Review: A Word About Testing

We've presented information just about testing, so let's review some key points. Remember that tests have two purposes:

As a feedback tool, tests can provide the facilitator with three useful pieces of information:

1. The degree to which goals have been achieved.

2. The degree to which participants will be successful on the job.

3. How effective the facilitator's teaching was.

As a learning device, tests aid retention and sometimes make relationships clear. They are especially effective for those types of learners who depend on hard facts and data because they want to see results. Learners who lean towards the observing and perceiving traits respond well to essay tests.

When should you test? Generally testing is most effective when administered at the end of teaching a section or group of performance goals. Some program facilitators will include a start-up quiz to get the participants involved in the performance goals immediately.

> I handed out post-tests during the last role play, when participants were in small groups. They all had them completed by the end of the wrap-up session. I graded them that week and followed up with each small group individually.

One learning device is to have participants take a test, score it themselves, and read through prepared feedback information. This method puts the participants in charge of their own learning process, which frequently increases learning. If you return the tests corrected and encourage questions on missed items, it will help clear up areas which may have been mislearned, partially learned, or not learned at all.

Summary: Key Points on Designing and Developing Your Training Program

Basic design skills

- Write clear, measurable goals.

- **Know how** the participants should apply the learning to the workplace so that what you teach is relevant.

- Use **time efficiently.** The group will want to question and discuss points along the way. However, do not use discussions as a filler; participants must be kept on track.

- **Variety is essential** and unpredictability is the key. People learn best when there is stimulation—even tension—which forces them to think and behave in ways that are not always familiar.

- **Use time as a design tool.** Time can be manipulated by establishing somewhat tight constraints, being sure to provide time for listening, discussing, and doing. Use different learning tools and mediums. Adults can typically digest only fifteen minutes of lecture, activities, or discussion before their attention drifts, so use your time wisely.

- **Plan for interaction.** Give the group opportunities to work as a whole and in smaller clusters. We'll get deeper into group interaction in the next chapter.

- **Vary the physical setting.** All learning does not need to occur behind tables in a classroom style.

- **Sequence information correctly.** Anticipate what kinds of experiences need to happen in what order.

Program development may be the most difficult task facing a facilitator. It can also be the most enjoyable, because this is where facilitators stamp their names on the program. With some creativity and willingness to update, alter, and improve, a facilitator can present a successful program.

Teaching Materials and Techniques

The next several pages are full of teaching materials, hints, applications—just about everything you need to round out the design and development of your training program. This list includes the following techniques:

1. Questions
- Direct questions
- Open-ended questions
- Reflective questions
- Hints on composing and using questions

2. Discussion
- Advantages and disadvantages

3. Lectures
- Developing a lecture
- Advantages and disadvantages
- Suggestions for better lectures

4. Role plays
- Multiple role plays
- Reversal
- Doubling
- Advantages and disadvantages
- Tips for conducting role plays

5. Audio and visual devices
- Chalkboards
- Overhead and slide projectors
- Tape recorder
- Videocassette recorder
- Charts and graphics

6. Case studies
- Setting up a fictional scenario
- When to use them

1. Questions

Questions are perhaps the most effective and popular technique facilitators have at their disposal. Let's examine three specific types of questions, some general rules for composing them and some hints on their use in your program.

Direct questions

This questioning technique allows you to direct group discussion. It also allows you to elicit responses from the greatest number of participants, while limiting the amount of input each one makes.

The purpose of the direct question is to:
- get specific answers.
- guide group discussion toward a specific problem.
- involve all members of the workshop.
- provide a clear idea of what you are after.
- provide a framework for summary statements.

Because the direct question is coercive and nonpermissive, it should be used with caution in an open discussion. It tends to force conclusions. It also puts the facilitator in the role of director and elicits a large number of "yes" and "no" answers.

> I asked my participants questions such as, "Is this is a constructive statement in a discussion with a supervisor: 'I feel like I do not have a distinctive or entirely specific job description.' Here's another question: "Who can find fault with this statement made to a supervisor? 'My job description stinks and I'm sick of it!' "

Open-ended questions

A question such as, "How do you feel about the service you receive when you go into a department store?" opens up the chance for sharing feelings. It cannot be answered by a "yes" or a "no." An open question is beneficial when you are not looking for a specific answer. Each answer gives you the potential chance to hitchhike on different ideas or feelings that have been expressed.

Open-ended questions can be used to:
- allow for a variety of viewpoints and answers.
- promote open and noncoercive participation.
- elicit the feelings participants have on certain subjects.
- promote productive disagreement.

Some things you will have to consider using this technique:
- It gives participants the chance to diverge from the topic, taking tangents that may not be related to the goals of your program.
- It allows some members to sit back and listen while other participants dominate.
- It sometimes causes confusion due to its unspecified nature.

> The open-ended question technique creates a friendly atmosphere and encourages good group discussion. One question I used was, "What's the best way to tell people you supervise that they need to change their attitude on the job?"

Reflective questions

The reflective question encourages further elaboration of a statement made by a participant. It may be a simple restatement, a repeated key word, or an interpretive restatement.

A simple statement of "I like to work at my computer station" could become, "You enjoy computer work?" or "Like to?" or "You enjoy the structure provided by the work?" It involves taking the statement and phrasing the basic content into a question.

> When Adam said something like, "The procedures done by students take way too long," I asked a couple of questions: "Not fast enough? Might there be too much pressure on the medical student taking the tubes out? What do you think?"

Hints on composing and using questions

- **Questions should be a challenge.** Unless you're testing factual knowledge, ask questions that tax more than the memory so participants have to apply facts that they've learned.

> Take individual differences into consideration. Material that challenges one participant may be too simple for another. Be sure to adapt the question to the level of the participant.
>
> I found that the new employees responded really well to yes/no questions, while some of my regulars felt confident enough to answer the lengthier ones.

- **Make the wording definite, clear, and concise.** Use clear language so the participants know exactly what you're asking. For example, words such as the following help indicate both the purpose and type of response the questioner seeks to: classify, define, illustrate, explain, interpret, summarize, compare, discuss, justify, and review.

- **Plan ahead.** In order to create effective questions and tests, you'll need to make question development a regular part of your program planning. When you need a key question to hold your participants' attention or develop a specific idea, you'll want it to be a good one.

- **Distribute questions fairly among the participants.** This doesn't mean that you have to ask each person an equal number of questions. You must be sure not to pick on any individual or allow one person to assume a star role.

- **Don't call on people in a fixed order.** The participants will soon learn the pattern and pay attention only when they're about to be called on.

- **Allow ample time for answering.** A few seconds may be enough if you're asking for a simple fact. If the goal is more than recall, encourage your participants to take some time to think about their replies. Also, some people require a bit more time to think about their answers before responding. It may help to ask people how they arrived at an answer.

- **Ask the question, then name the participant.** Address the question to the entire group before you choose someone to respond. Remember, as soon as you direct the question to one person, you'll lose the close attention of the others. Ask the question first!

- **Ask only one question at a time.** If a participant does not answer you right away, wait until he or she asks you to repeat the question before you ask it again. By rephrasing, you may seem to be asking another question, and people may get flustered or upset. Tandem questions lead to confusion, not conclusion.

- **Encourage good answers.** Praise motivates. Remember that people learn at different rates, so try to praise any answers that are good according to ability and not necessarily the speed of the response.

- **Use questions to keep participants alert.** Asking questions will encourage participation. A question may remedy the inattention you sense during a lecture or discussion. Always remember, ask questions in order to get attention and not in order to embarrass.

- **Do not permit group answers.** After stating the question, call on one person by name so that you get a single response, not a chorus. If your participants answer all at once, you'll hear only the loudest responses, or none at all.

That's a lot of information just on questions, so don't try to incorporate it all at once. Get a feel for what types of questions your participants respond well to, which are not always the kinds of questions that elicit the best answers.

2. Discussion Techniques

Group discussion develops the flow of ideas between facilitators and participants. It's usually directed toward a particular goal, but often is used just to get ideas rolling. Discussion encourages a high level of participation and is a great way to obtain new ideas, to solve specific problems, and to iron out gripes.

When deciding on discussion topics, remember that your main goal is communication. Plan your kick-off remarks, the comments you intend to make, and the questions you plan to ask only after you've decided on the tone of your program.

Ask these questions about your participants before you engage them in any discussions:

- Do they have enough factual background to make worthwhile contributions?

- Could their perceptions be broadened or opened by discussion?

- Will they be free to express themselves in front of the other people who will be present?

> I found that a good discussion can really help the morale of the group, especially if you've got a few opinionated people who are willing to vigorously debate a point. Just remember to control the swing of the discussion so it doesn't get off track with statements like, "Remember our goal now . . . let's keep the discussion centered around . . ."

Discussion does have some drawbacks; it's an ineffective way to convey specific information such as system operation or company policies.

> Here is an example of when discussion isn't very helpful. In most hospitals, specific guidelines control how cases that need special equipment are prioritized. The equipment is always supposed to be used on the most crucial cases. You could discuss it forever, but that won't change the hospital policy.

3. Lectures

Lectures are formal discourses in which facilitators develop the subject without audience participation. This method makes the facilitator solely responsible for planning, presenting, and supporting the presentation, and for the direction and depth of the ideas presented. Its success depends upon effective speaking skills, but many other factors contribute.

Through a lecture, you may present a large amount of information (usually background information) to many people at one time. Of course, there are some situations in which a lecture would be all wrong: with small groups, for instance, which generally crave interaction.

Here is a simple format guide to help you to get started:

- **Select one general idea.** This is a capsule summary of the presentation's theme. Every other idea will illustrate or support this central idea. Draw on your goals as you select your main theme.

- **Select the basic supporting ideas.** These are the major planks upon which the basic theme rests. They are the proofs, the explanations, and the reasons that establish your position.

- **Select details to bolster the supporting ideas.** Use facts, illustrations, quotations, anecdotes, and stories. By locating and making good use of supporting material, you'll set your program apart from those in which employees simply gather to hear company manuals or new regulations read aloud.

- **Plan an introduction.** It must arouse interest, then accurately direct your participants' attention to your subject. This should comprise about 25 percent of your lecturing time.

- **Plan the body with a clearly stated thesis.** Use a key points outline and write an outline of the lecture. If you include this sheet as a handout, your participants will pay better attention. This should comprise about 70 percent of your lecturing time.

- **Plan a conclusion.** Summarize the main points, remembering to direct your participants visually by either mental images or visual aids.

Keep asking yourself these questions as you are planning your lecture: Am I balancing my material between general and specific examples? Am I offering visual stimuli as well as verbal and intellectual stimuli?

4. Role Plays

Role-playing is a way to train your participants in realistic behavior under unrealistic conditions—substituting a variety of contrived situations for actual on-the-job behavior. The role-player acts as if the situation were real. For example: as the facilitator, you wish to demonstrate good telephone answering techniques. You ask a participant to be the caller, arrange a desk and phone for the person who is answering the phone—role-playing is underway.

Role plays do not need to be formal or complicated. Simply asking a participant to respond to an imagined situation as if it were real is effective role-playing. If you want to use role-playing to change the attitudes of your participants, there are several techniques which you should know and use.

Multiple role plays

These involve the entire group. Instead of having one cast of characters acting out a situation in front of the remaining members, all members act simultaneously in small groups. This is an effective way of involving everyone and overcoming the shyness of quiet members. It will also get the attention of the group prior to a presentation which uses more conventional training methods.

Reversal

"Reversal" simply involves having participants switch characters in the middle of the role play. It is an excellent method of learning how other people feel about the way we act and allows participants to gain a whole new perspective on a situation. This method fosters change in participants' attitude very well.

Doubling

To "double" in role-playing, let all interested participants get involved by taking turns in the role. This is a kind of brainstorming in which the participants try out different ways of handling a situation.

We didn't have much discussion about trauma ward techniques, but we did role-play some of the most stressful issues, such as group interaction on a trauma case. You could tell who had experience in this area; they were the ones who wanted to keep on going.

You'll find that role plays foster high interest levels. Participants get very involved, and this in turn sparks thought and discussion. Role-playing is concrete; thus it makes tangible topics such as courtesy, which are hard to teach by lecture or discussion. When people see these concepts at work in role plays, the terms become more meaningful.

You will probably find that role plays can be hard to stop once participants get started. Just know that the situation need not be acted out to its final conclusion. You can call a halt as soon as the participants have illustrated the basic point you wanted to make.

Tips for conducting role plays

- Keep the role play scenarios initially simple and low key. Simply describe a situation up to a given point, then prompt the scene.

- Don't select the "hams" to act in the first role play.

- Warm up with multiple role plays.

- Arrange your participants in a circle, with no furniture between them.

- Interrupt whenever participants have reached the goal of the role play or strayed from the point.

- If you ask for replies to questions "in character," see that participants do so as well. They'll soon get into the swing of it.

- Sometimes you'll want to use a more structured role play to be certain that participants will arrive at your goal. When this is the case, you will have to offer enough information for them to play the role completely. Carefully plan and organize the roles beforehand, describing the role and the situation on paper, up to the point at which the participants will begin the role play. During the program, you can hand the written description to the players and let them take over.

5. Visual and Audio Aids

Visual and audio aids provide a link between concept and comprehension. Facilitators and participants are both aware that verbalization alone will not produce the most meaningful, effective learning situation.

A visual or audio aid is any device or piece of equipment that helps participants understand a subject. Aids do not replace the facilitator nor do they reduce work. However, they do support, supplement, and reinforce the facilitator.

Program content can be made more realistic and interesting by the use of visual aids. Good design and proper use of color and animation give vivid, intense impressions. Visual aids help participants focus attention on one item—at the right time.

Many aids are available to facilitators. Each one has its advantages and disadvantages. When selecting aids, remember that they are only tools to help you achieve your goals. An inappropriate aid or one that is chosen only to overwhelm, fascinate, or beguile the participants will hinder learning, not help it. A well-chosen aid will produce desired results within the limitations of the program.

To avoid unpleasant surprises, give yourself plenty of time to check any equipment you plan to use. And be prepared with alternatives, so the presentation can go on even if the electricity goes off.

> Visual aids don't have to be fancy. I didn't have much equipment available to me, but my session seemed to flow pretty well with the use of a chalkboard, which I knew would be available in the classroom.

The most commonly used visual aids are the chalkboard, the overhead projector, the slide projector, the tape recorder, the VCR, and handouts.

Chalkboards and easel pads

The versatility and effectiveness of the chalkboard and easel pad make them valuable aids to most programs. They provide an easy way to record immediate information and to present prepared materials.

To use the chalkboard effectively, you should do the following:

- Plan your chalkboard work and your lesson plan together. Organize and practice the presentation in advance.

- Keep the chalkboard clean—make certain that chalk or fresh markers and a clean eraser will be available.

- Keep all irrelevant or unwanted material erased during your presentation.

- Use that part of the chalkboard which all participants can see without difficulty. Be alert for windows which throw too much sun or reflections on the board.

- Print and draw quickly—your lines will be straighter!

- Use several colors for emphasis, but don't overdo it!

- Make your writing and drawing large, clear, and legible.

- Do not overcrowd—leave a margin around material and space between lines of copy.

- Prepare intricate diagrams in advance, then cover them until you're ready to present them.

- Use some sort of pointer which will allow you to stand away from the board. If you're too close, you'll block the view.

- Don't talk into the board. You'll lose eye contact and cut the volume of your voice.

Overhead projector

Overhead projectors combine some good features of both the slide projector and the chalkboard. They project a large image behind the facilitator. They can present the material that you would ordinarily put onto a chalkboard as well as more professionally prepared charts, diagrams, and drawings. You can alter or make additions to the transparency while it is being projected by using a grease pencil and an erasing cloth. You can use the machine and still face the participants. Room lights can be left on so participants can see their notes.

The overhead projector will be effective if you:

- Select or prepare transparencies which will help to emphasize or illustrate major points of the presentation.

- Arrange the transparencies so that they're in the correct order for your presentation.

- Plan your comments for each projected view. Review each transparency and make sure you understand them before you present them at the program.

- Make sure the lights in the room are adjusted and the machine is focused before the program begins.

- Make sure all the participants can see the screen clearly.

- Vary your routine by using a pointer on the transparency; hold the pointer steadily (or lay it on the bed of the screen) and move it slowly.

- Remember that what is ineffective, unsatisfactory, or unexciting on paper is seldom improved by making it into a transparency.

- Refrain from reading your transparency during the program. If you do, you'll evade the purpose of using visuals. Shaking this natural tendency takes practice.

Slide projector or computer with a presentation program

Slide projectors are suitable for almost all training done today. The rapid pace of change in companies and industries requires a constant process of updating employees and letting them know "what's new." The slide projector can be effective for providing those updates. With tape narration and sound effects, a slide program can tell a story, present a concept, or teach new ideas.

Before using the slide projector, be aware that it does have drawbacks:

- You'll be working in a darkened room, and it will be difficult for both you and the participants to see any written material. This can be remedied with a soft light at the rear of the room, which won't interfere with the visibility of the projected image.

- A long procession of slides can grow monotonous. People often get bored when given the same type of stimulus too often.

- If commercially produced, slides can be quite expensive.

- Time can also be a problem. You must plan in advance to have enough time to prepare the slides.

- If you are using a computer and a presentation program, such as PowerPoint, be sure to allow plenty of time to test your equipment, software, and files.

Tape recorder

The tape recorder captures and provides feedback that can be valuable for both the trainer and participants.

The tape recorder has many training uses:

- Narration and sound effects can improve the effectiveness of slide programs.

- A presentation can be made by using a recorded voice and a series of charts or overhead projector transparencies.

- You can record an entire program and play it back for study, reference, or review.

- Recordings increase interest, as a variety of voices and sounds may be introduced to the training situation.

- Tapes can save the facilitator much tiresome repetition.

- Tapes are excellent for presenting case studies. At any point in the case, the tape may be stopped for group discussion.

- Recordings help greatly in developing public contact skills. By listening to themselves on tape, participants can work on improving their voices and speaking styles. So can facilitators!

- Recorders can bring the "voice of authority" to your program. While company managers and executives cannot always be present during a program, you would probably have little trouble enlisting their support by tape.

When using tape recorders:

- Have the equipment ready to go before the program begins. Be sure you are familiar with the operation of the particular machine you will be using.

- Have the tape positioned in the machine at the point where you wish to begin.

- Preset the volume, remembering that it will be affected by factors such as the number of people in the room, heat blowers, and other extraneous noise that may require adjustment during the presentation. You want everyone to hear, but be careful not to make it irritatingly loud.

Videotape player

The videotape is a very effective aid when your goal is to show action or tell a story. It is helpful in demonstrating how something works or how a procedure is done. It can show motion, relationships, sequences, practices, and techniques—things which are difficult to describe orally.

Some important suggestions when using videotapes are:

- Select the tape carefully. Be sure it serves a definite and logical purpose.

- Always preview the tape before showing it to a group. This enables you to plan your program, pick out the high points and prepare comments and questions so you can capitalize on the content of the tape.

- Prepare the participants for the video by explaining its purpose. List on the blackboard the title of the video and the main points that should be observed.

- Prepare the room, placing the VCR and seats so all can easily see.

- Always remain in the room while the video is running. People will lose interest and get distracted if you leave.

- Discuss the main points in the video after the showing. This may be done by asking questions about the content or how the content may be applied. These questions should be prepared while you are previewing the video.

- Test your participants if the video offers specific data which your participants should know.

- Explore the possibility of showing some videos more than once to the same group. This device can be especially productive when there is a plot in the video. The emotional involvement produced by the story can frequently permit more than one analysis of the video content, each on a different level.

Handouts

Give participants something to help them recall your presentation. Even if they take careful notes, they are likely to miss some of the points you want them to remember. Complex material presented in tables, charts, and graphs will not be remembered without the help of handouts.

An outline of the presentation lets everyone know what to anticipate and helps them focus on your main points. Distribute it at the beginning of the session.

Consider carefully whether other handouts should be distributed before, during, or after the session. If you give them out too early, you may find that participants are reading their handouts instead of listening to your presentation. On the other hand, they may need to make notes directly on charts and graphs.

Charts are an effective way to present facts, directions, procedures, and illustrations.

Some types of charts and general applications are:

- **Pie Chart:** This graph shows the division of a total area into segments.

- **Bar Graph:** This graph directly compares various elements to one another.

- **Pictorial Chart:** This chart makes use of figures which represent the items being discussed—pictographs of people, equipment, etc.

- **Curve-Angle Chart:** This chart makes use of single line curves and angles to illustrate rises and falls, peaks and valleys, and input-output relationships.

Here are a few tips on designing and making use of charts and graphs:

- Do not use charts which present more ideas than the participants can understand in a short period of time. Charts showing too many steps of a process at once should be broken into a series of simpler charts, each showing only one part of the process.

- Select and prepare charts which use color to emphasize important features whenever possible.

- Make sure YOU understand the charts or graphs you are using.

- Plan your verbal presentation to make the best use of the chart.

- Store all the graphics that aren't being used where people can't see them. Added charts or diagrams create a cluttered atmosphere and distract attention from the current agenda.

- Make sure everyone can see the chart you are using. Stand to one side when you talk. Use a pointer if necessary.

- Keep the aids simple.

- Make your lines thick enough to be seen clearly from a distance.

- Use key words (as few as possible) and art. Graphics which carry only words are really only "visual-verbals."

The design and development portion of your program is now done. Hopefully the session you intend to give has shape and can stand on its own as a training program. Now, a question: What is the number one fear of most people? Public speaking. I tried to convince the nurses that the emergency room was nothing compared to presenting this program! Although there are ways to make it easier . . .

Stand
and Deliver

Knowing all about what you want to teach is only half the job, albeit an important half. Of course you must be well versed in your subject matter—so well versed that you can tell anyone about it. That's what this chapter is all about: the techniques and skills needed to communicate information, skills, and behaviors in a way that will cause change.

There is no model for a "perfect" facilitator. Training involves an intensive extension of the self to the learners, and since we are all different, we all train or facilitate differently. We have included many techniques, methods, and suggestions for instructing, but it is up to you to establish your own identity as a trainer.

We begin by describing a set of communication skills. Your role is outlined, as well as requirements for being an excellent facilitator. Group dynamics are explained, and you'll have a chance to write out your version of the ideal facilitator.

Next we'll bring you back to earth with the barriers and pitfalls that may come your way. Being prepared for these potential hazards will boost your confidence.

Don't worry, while delivering a program is not easy, working through this chapter is. Just follow along and keep your mind open. Everything will be explained.

Then we'll describe some of the basic facilitating styles in Chapter 13, Effective Communication Techniques. And finally, an application section will assist you in applying the principles and concepts of this chapter. An action plan is included for you to record what you wish to change or strengthen upon finishing this chapter.

The basics of communication

The three most basic rules of communication are:

1. **Prepare carefully.** Organize what you are going to talk about. Hopefully the first two sections of this book helped you with this prerequisite.

2. **Know your group.** Understand their needs and wants as well as their backgrounds and what brings them to the session. Again, sections one and two cover this.

3. **Use a wide variety of techniques and skills.** Your understanding of people and relationships and how each impacts the communication process will affect how you put your ideas across.

See, it's simple. You just need to know what you are talking about, who you are talking to, and how to get it across. Now, how exactly *do* you get it across?

11

Ideally . . .

As an effective facilitator, you must draw on a wide repertoire of behaviors. At any given moment, you may be direct, persuasive, humorous, outrageous, quiet, noisy, confrontational, self-disclosing, supportive, nonemotional, or angry—whatever is called for at that particular time, whatever is right and responsive to the needs of the situation.

You are directly responsible for making connections between the learner and the information or content in the program. This synergy is necessary for a positive and productive outcome.

Six ways to ensure good communication

1. **Maintain a climate of mutual respect and trust.** People must feel that their experiences are valued and that they are spoken to as equals. Each group member needs to feel that he or she is important to the whole.

2. **Attempt to form a warm, friendly relationship with group members.** However, any fears you have of hostile expressions should not cause participants to repress their feelings or inhibit healthy conflict. Your needs cannot interfere with the helping-learning process.

3. **Accept and listen to each individual.** This includes learners who lack knowledge, abilities, and effective learning skills. Develop helpful relationships with all group members.

4. **Be aware of group dynamics so that you can skillfully lead the group.** This will help you to understand stages of group development, individualize within the group, minimize scapegoating, and handle intergroup conflict.

5. **Remind the group of the goals to be attained.** Be able to specify learning goals consistent with learners' needs and to describe specific outcomes.

6. **Encourage participants to focus on what they are learning.** With adult learners, it is important to identify ways to apply new knowledge, develop plans to use it, and consider how they might successfully confront obstacles to implementing what they have learned.

I found that by sometimes talking with an individual as if we were in a normal conversation, I was in a good position to find effective communication avenues. This is individualizing.

The basics of group dynamics

The learning process in any program takes place in a group. An unspoken learning contract exists between the facilitator, the participant, and the group itself as a learning entity.

The group is a very powerful force that either supports or detracts from the learning process. The function of the group should be to support the learning process of its members. As a facilitator you need to assume responsibility for the growth and maintenance of the group. An effective facilitator sets the climate and conditions under which the group can build and grow and encourages free expression and a group sense of well being.

This was especially critical for the younger employees (mostly orderlies) in my session. I really had to make sure they felt free enough to ask questions, voice concerns, and such. I ended up setting aside a time, before I moved on to the next main point, to ask these new people some specific questions, such as "Is this the way you would do this?" or "Tell me what you think about that last point."

A group develops into a cohesive learning unit after a series of phases supported and encouraged by the facilitator. There are many theories on the stages a group goes through, and countless ways you can communicate and design a workshop or program for a group to help them get to the most constructive stage.

The facilitator as a change agent

Change: the goal of every workshop or program. It requires that a new skill, process, or behavior be learned and put into action.

Change of any kind creates a certain amount of resistance or skepticism; that is a natural part of the change process. You are likely to encounter opposition. Depending upon the amount of change you need or expect from your participants, you'll probably encounter some degree of resistance.

Individuals accept changes in ideas or techniques at three different levels: compliance, identification, and internalization.

Compliance is the most superficial level of acceptance; it occurs when an individual follows the facilitator's advice simply to gain a reward or to avoid punishment. Compliant individuals have little understanding of the rationale behind the strategies they are learning. As a result, they perform the required behaviors only during the workshop session or when under supervision.

> Some of the younger employees seemed to like this when the session first started. They just said, "Yeah, uh-huh" to almost everything I said. I even told them that they were not allowed to talk ever again in this hospital, and they said, "Yeah, uh-huh."

A greater degree of acceptance occurs at the level of identification. At this level, individuals try suggested strategies to establish or maintain a satisfying relationship with the facilitator advocating the technique. It is not unusual for participants to adopt certain behaviors because they admire the person suggesting them. Eventually, individuals who use a technique for this reason may come to believe in it and understand why it is useful. Still, their actions are based on their high regard for the person promoting the behavior rather than their own analysis of the strategy. Participants at this level tend to adopt behaviors for a short period of time but revert to old habits when no longer in direct contact with the facilitator.

I think some of the young employees saw how my employees respect my supervision, and then they really started to listen to me. Watch for the way some people do this. They learn a lot from each other.

The third and most complete level of acceptance is called internalization. Internalization occurs when individuals consider the suggested strategy to be an extension of their own beliefs. The new method may be very different from their usual practices, but the goals match those they have already established for themselves. On this level, individuals examine new ideas very carefully and commit themselves to using the new ideas because they seem to provide a logical method for attaining their personal goals. As a result, they are able to make the new strategy a natural part of their own behavior. They are also likely to continue using the new method back on the job.

Many of my nurses were reluctant to try role-playing, because they already have tenuous relationships with each other. So, I explained to them that I felt that role-playing could be an effective tool for understanding stress-management. They agreed to give it a try, and it worked.

The "Ideal" Facilitator

Answer the questions as honestly as you can. Write down the first response that comes to mind as you read the questions. Do not edit!

1. What have you seen a facilitator do that helped a group's learning?

_____

_____

_____

2. What have you seen a facilitator do that hindered a group's learning?

_____

_____

_____

3. What can a facilitator do to create a learning environment that is both comfortable and stimulating?

_____

_____

_____

4. What kinds of things would an "ideal" facilitator say and do?

_____

_____

_____

_____

_____

_____

Visualizing the interactive relationship

A unique relationship takes place between learners and facilitators.

Learners bring:

- perceptions about their needs and their ability to learn.

- concepts about the way learning should take place for them.

- filters or screens that distort the communication process.

- different levels of interpersonal skills.

Facilitators bring:

- awareness of the basic teaching/learning process.

- their own needs and motivations.

- the ability to accept participants as individuals.

- skills in group leadership and membership.

When combined, the resulting goals of this interaction are:

- to establish and maintain relationships which can help reduce participant anxieties and defensiveness.

- to bring about learning and change.

Meanwhile, Back in the Real World . . .

We all know that things seldom go as smoothly as planned. Of course, armed with the knowledge that this lesson will impart to you, things might go better! Let's review the five stages of group interaction, then assess some of the pitfalls of communicating to a group.

The five stages of group interaction

The five stages of group interaction are based on "Cogs Ladder," a model first introduced in 1972 in the *Advanced Management Journal (Vol. 34, No. 1)*. We've added some ideas to help facilitators communicate with the group during each stage.

1. Polite stage

During this stage, group members get acquainted, share values, and make small talk. At this stage, participants need to be motivated. Asking questions of them is helpful.

Communication ideas:

- Have participants introduce themselves and perhaps tell something of their back-grounds.

- Include an opening activity that will get people talking to each other, as individuals or in small groups, about their goals and about their hopes for the session.

- Encourage each person to share information about themselves.

> I encouraged everyone to take a few minutes and tell us where they're from and what kind of nursing they do, along with any other information they wish to share.

2. Why we're here stage

During this phase the group participants want to know the goals of the session. Some people need them in writing, while others may prefer a detailed discussion.

Communication ideas:

- Post the objectives on a chart or distribute a handout.

- Present and provide justification for each objective.

> One thing that would help is to be clear on what can be accomplished during your session and what can not. If one participant has a special need or goal, meet with them individually to offer help.

3. Bid for power stage

At this stage, group members attempt to influence one another's ideas, values, or opinions. This stage is characterized by competition for attention, recognition, and influence. Conflict may arise, causing some participants to feel uncomfortable. In response, some may become silent; others may become louder. Hidden agendas frequently surface at this time.

Communication ideas:

- At this stage, you may use discussion, compromise, or arbitration to handle the participants.

- If participants are working in a small group, have them select a spokesperson if the need for structure is strong.
  - Allow the leaders of small groups to share the group's ideas and thoughts.
  - Give equal speaking time to each participant; use an actual timer or your watch.

- The facilitator may switch from harmonizer to compromiser to gatekeeper, but must always be balanced and fair.
  - Deal with facts; recognize feelings; then restate facts.
  - Keep the group on track—remind participants of their goals and the goals for each discussion.
  - Change pace. For example, go from small group to large group discussion, or from lecture to exercise.
  - Take a break.
  - Deal with an especially concerned or demanding participant one-on-one.

Make sure participants express themselves using the phrases "I feel" or "I think," rather than "you do."

> You may not be able to deal with all the conflicts that arise. That's fine. Give people an opportunity to express themselves, and then move on—explaining why this is necessary. The ability to listen is the most important skill to take your group from stage 3 to 4.

4. The constructive stage

In this phase, participants are open minded. They listen actively and can accept the fact that others have a right to different value systems.

Communication ideas:

- Use any group activity at this time that includes sharing, listening, questioning, or building.

- Ask constructive questions, summarize and clarify points.

- Reinforce and encourage positive and varied contributions to the group's goals.

- Avoid introducing competitive exercises at this time.

5. The unified stage

At this phase, spirits are high. The group feels unified and cohesive, and there is mutual acceptance. Morale is good and group loyalty is high.

Communication ideas:

- Encourage creativity and involvement.

- Be constructive and productive.

- Supply materials, information, and goals, as well as guidelines and timing. The group will complete their tasks and come to you with questions.

- Ask questions spontaneously to heighten involvement. You will have good attention if you try lecturing at this time.

Out of our group of 35 people, 10 hardly ever spoke up. I was worried that they were feeling left out and would report that in their assessments at the end of the session. I handled this problem in a couple of ways. One way was to directly deal with the process, the group dynamic. So I said, "I keep hearing from many of the same people. Any ideas about how everyone might more evenly participate so as not to leave anyone out?"

The three pitfalls

If you facilitate groups regularly, you're bound to run into some difficult and disruptive participants. Disruptive behaviors displayed in the classroom fall into three main categories: withdrawal, diversion, and attack.

1. **Withdrawal** is the refusal to actively participate. Withdrawal takes two forms: apathy and hostility. Apathy is demonstrated by daydreaming, token participation in group activities and discussions, and lack of response to questions. Hostility takes the form of blatantly ignoring the trainer, refusing to respond to questions, and refusing to participate in a group's activities and discussions.

2. **Diversion** occurs when participants initiate side discussions with others in the room, work on other material, clean their fingernails, look out the windows, dominate the discussion on some point minimally related to the original topic, or redirect the topic of discussion altogether. The list of diversionary tactics is endless.

   While serious students may at times ask silly or irrelevant questions, it should be obvious from their tone of voice and previous performance in class whether they're trying to disrupt the facilitator's presentation.

3. **Attack** is a direct challenge to the authority of the trainer. Attacking individuals will blatantly criticize the trainer, the subject matter, or the program. They may question the competency of the trainer directly, openly criticize training strategies or the agency itself. They may refuse to cooperate or argue about the information presented.

This kind of disruptive behavior often leads to confrontations, anger, and hostility on both sides. Times like these require the trainer to demonstrate diplomacy and conflict resolution skills. The impact of disruptive behavior on participants depends upon the trainer's personality, training approach and style, and upon the training environment itself.

How to reduce disruptive behavior

- **Treat the participants as adults, not as children.** Participants are often peers of the facilitator. Treat them with the respect they deserve and acknowledge the value of their contributions. Adults have background and experience, and they get defensive when that's ignored or slighted. Avoid such remarks as "How are we doing today, class?" Don't be condescending; an arrogant tone can be picked up right away, and nothing is as degrading to students as being talked down to. Have participants wear tags with their first names in large type so you can address them personally.

- **Make eye contact with everyone in the room.** Don't use a systematic pattern. Look at each person and maintain eye contact for longer than the usual three to five seconds. Talk with, not to, participants. Tilt your head toward people, walk around, listen to what they have to say. A good training session should teach the facilitator almost as much as the students.

- **Set up the room carefully** with a seating arrangement that allows you to personalize the instruction. A horseshoe arrangement allows for more intimacy than rows of desks and chairs. It allows participants to see each other and encourages interaction.

- **Be positive and nondefensive in your demeanor.** Don't try to play the role of expert or "know-it-all." Allow participants time to contribute. Be open to what they have to say. You will learn from them, and your openness will make them feel much more comfortable and relaxed in class. Be enthusiastic and positive. An enthusiastic leader makes for enthusiastic followers.

- **Ignore the disruptive behavior** if it's not distracting to the other people in the group. Lack of reinforcement may cause the behavior to disappear. Making it an issue may draw additional attention to it and cause the behavior to be rewarded rather than discouraged.

- **Talk to disruptive people privately.** During breaks in the session, pull the disruptive participants aside and try to discover what is causing their behavior. A two-minute discussion can save you hours of headaches.

You know what I did? I moved closer to the disruptive people. I made eye contact and I held it. The closer I got to the people who were chatting, the more they had to pay attention to me and what I was saying.

The relationship you develop with individual participants will have a great effect on their behavior. The quality of those relationships will also determine whether the group will support your efforts to control any disruptive behavior that may occur. Be very conscious of your attitude and demeanor so that positive interpersonal relationships develop.

Although a conscientious effort to develop positive interpersonal relationships makes it less likely that problems will occur, it cannot ensure that disruptive behavior will never erupt. If you're prepared, you won't be surprised—so plan your problem solving strategies in advance.

Now I think we've spent quite enough time on problems. The question is, how can we suit you up to deal with all this? Assess your current inventory of communication skills on the next page.

Communication Skills Inventory

It is critical for facilitators to recognize that the group process is a delicate human exchange requiring skill and sensitivity in human relations. The following worksheet will provide you with information about your training style and skills.

Read the beginning phrases and choose the letter next to the phrase that best describes your facilitating style.

> If you have never been a facilitator, then choose the ending you think would describe how you might behave. There are no right answers, so go with your first choice.

1. In my program, I feel I create an atmosphere in which:
   a. feelings and emotions are acceptable.
   b. the participants use their senses to experience new information.
   c. the participants learn by understanding relationships and associations between the new information and their previous knowledge.
   d. people act and respond to learning stimulation.

2. In my program, I:
   a. encourage participants to evaluate their own progress.
   b. encourage participants to memorize foundational theories, terms, and guidelines.
   c. take charge of the learning and direct the activities.
   d. encourage participants to freely express their needs and wants.

3. During the program or learning session, I:
   a. give immediate personal feedback to each participant, as necessary.
   b. use discipline, rules, external criteria, and guidelines to evaluate how everyone is doing.
   c. encourage the participants to use their judgment to evaluate things.
   d. make use of goal criteria as a means to evaluate.

4. As a way to learn, I feel:
   a. discussion among participants is the best method.
   b. it is important that participants know terms and rules in order to learn.
   c. that participants need to be self-directed and free to express their personal needs.
   d. participants have to make maximum use of notes, outlines, and goals.

5. The learning techniques I am most comfortable with are:
   a. case studies, lectures, resource articles, and books.
   b. lectures, with good examples and well organized plans.
   c. role plays, actual projects that reflect participants' realities, and simulations.
   d. group discussions, activities, and interactive experiences.

6. The rapport I like to have with my participants is:
   a. sharing and expressing feelings.
   b. active and interactive.
   c. little, but directive.
   d. encouraging and interpretive.

7. When facilitating, I focus on:
   a. the present and current needs of participants.
   b. "how" things get done and "why" they are done this way.
   c. past theories and their interpretation for today.
   d. what will work in real life and how it will work.

8. I believe that learning best takes place:
   a. by concentrating on models and illustrations.
   b. between and among participants in a workshop.
   c. when participants act out new skills and behaviors.
   d. through a thorough understanding of facts and terminology.

Worksheet: Inventory Scoring

Go back to each completed phrase, then locate and circle your responses on this worksheet.

	A.				T.	
1. a		5. c		1. c		5. a
2. d		6. a		2. b		6. d
3. a		7. a		3. d		7. c
4. c		8. b		4. b		8. d

	C.				P.	
1. d		5. d		1. b		5. b
2. a		6. b		2. c		6. c
3. c		7. d		3. b		7. b
4. a		8. c		4. d		8. a

Now match the choices you made to the communication styles described on the following page. Are your characteristics all in one box or spread out? Read all the style descriptions, then come back to these pages when it is time to plan for those skills you want to strengthen or change. This information will help you identify a style or facilitator trait you want or need to use more often.

Effective Communication Techniques

The features characteristic of the four most common communication styles are described below. As you will see, each style has certain benefits. Use this information to build on the strengths of your style.

{A} Attender

- encourages expression of needs and feelings
- takes care of each participant
- reads body language well
- fosters self-direction and autonomy
- empathizes with participants

> Mothers are great attenders. Come to think of it, attenders are great mothers. They really foster trust, often phrasing statements from the attendee's point of view: "How did that make you feel?"

{T} Translator

- encourages participants to learn theory, terms, and rules
- shares ideas and goal data
- welcomes participant thoughts
- fosters independent thinking based on fact
- observes participants

> I'm definitely a translator. I use examples a lot, and I'm convinced I need to use more. During the session I said to a new employee: "Here's how I solved this. But show me how YOU would."

{C} Coach

- encourages involvement and self-evaluation
- promotes experimentation as long as results are practical
- fosters applying of group resources
- helps participants tap their own strengths
- supporter

My supervisor is always telling us to pool our thoughts. This is a lot like a football coach saying huddle up.

{P} Pilot

- takes charge and gives direction
- well-organized and prepared, uses goal criteria to evaluate, sets limits and controls participation, concentrates on detail

Now that you have an idea of what your facilitator orientation is, you are probably also aware of the fact that no one technique or strategy is good all the time.

Review the choices you made and the different ways there are to facilitate and make a conscious effort to use alternative styles to aid learning.

Analyzing communication techniques

This guide analyzes the three communication tools facilitators most often use. It identifies the skill, gives examples and ways to use it successfully, and points out the pros and cons of that specific technique. First we'll cover speaking, then questioning techniques, and finally listening as a feedback tool.

Speaking

1. State your ideas.

Pros: Takes least amount of time. Gives the greatest control.

Cons: Can become boring. Not everyone may get it!

2. Use examples.

Pros: Fun. Can be drawn from personal experience. Helpful to have one for each major point.

Cons: Example/story may overshadow point.

3. Demonstrate.

Pros: Can be an exciting and convincing way to practice what you want to teach.

Cons: Takes a lot of time. May evoke a lot of time-consuming questions.

4. Use your voice as a tool.

Pros: Using volume and pacing can call attention to certain points. Pausing after a word or thought can really help emphasize the idea.

Cons: Exaggerated vocal mannerisms will call attention to you rather than the information you are presenting.

5. Project a personal attitude.

Be yourself; your presentation should be a natural reflection of your personality.

Concentrate on ideas, not just words; this will help you avoid using jargon.

Extemporize, don't memorize; use the outline you designed in Chapter Two rather than a written text. Practice by doing a few dry runs in front of the mirror or with a tape recorder.

Pros: A relaxed, natural presentation will keep participants interested.

Cons: Don't simplify so much that important concepts are lost. If you simplify too much, participants may doubt your expertise and credibility or may believe that you're talking down to them.

Questioning

One of the most effective ways to communicate information is by getting participants to say it for you. The techniques for getting this to happen fall under two headings: questioning and listening.

The questions you ask must be accurate and useful. They should lead participants to the conclusion or idea you want to get across.

1. Ask direct questions.

The questions that first come to mind begin with: is, shall, do, will, can, has. They tend to elicit a "yes" or "no" response.

> Is there something wrong in the department?
> Do you think this is the correct procedure?
> Have we reached an agreement?

Pros: It takes little time to ask questions and get an answer.

Cons: Thought and communication are discouraged.

2. Ask open-ended questions.

These are questions which begin with: what, who, when, where, how, which.

They require more thought than questions that can be answered with "yes" and "no" and are more conducive to constructive elaboration.

What can you tell me about the atmosphere in the department?
How would you perform this procedure?
What can I do to help?

Pros: Use to solicit complete answers that rely on the ability of the person answering to convey relevant information.

Cons: Answers may move the discussion into unanticipated areas.

3. Ask follow-up questions.

Respond to answers in ways that convey interest and encourage people to keep talking.

What can you tell me about the situation?
Be a little more specific.
Give an example.

4. Ask questions that check meaning and interpretations. They show that you are trying to understand.

If I understand correctly, you do not think the procedure is practical. For what other reasons do you think it will not work?

5. Ask questions that show you understand how the speaker feels.

I see what you're saying. How can we make it better?

See, these are very basic questions, from a very basic theory: VARY the way you ask questions to your group, and you will be surprised how many different answers you can get!

Listening

Listening to your group takes a lot more than just opening your ears and hearing what they have to say. You're obviously going to be interested in what they have to say; the key is to complete the transaction. Let them know you understand.

1. Restate.

Restate all or part of a person's last sentence, or the basic idea in order to show the participant you are listening and understand what is being said. It also encourages the person to talk more freely.

> If I understand correctly, you feel . . .
> Let me see if I understand, you believe . . .

2. Paraphrase.

This technique involves more active participation on the facilitator's part; it takes effort to find the essence of what is said rather than simply mirroring words. It conveys to participants that you are trying to understand what they are saying. It crystallizes a participant's comment by making it more concise and also serves as a check on the accuracy of the facilitator's perceptions.

> Adam: "I do not know about this stress technique. For some people it's relaxing, but for me it's really aggravating."
> ME: "You think it's pretty inconsistent then."

3. Summarize.

Gather ideas and feelings, then restate them for participants in order to help them pull their thoughts together, prepare for further discussion, or gain perspective on problems.

> "Okay, Amy thinks it would make more sense to follow up with patients' families after all trauma ward decisions have been made, and she definitely thinks the clerks rather than the nurses should translate for families . . ."

4. Reflect feelings.

This technique is similar to restating, but focuses on reflecting the feelings participants express in order to demonstrate comprehension.

> "So, Henriette, you feel like most of the nurses under your supervision have their own way of doing things and won't listen to you? What about your newly learned stress-management techniques?"

5. Respond to nonverbal cues.

Show understanding by observing nonverbal cues and making comments or asking questions to clarify their meaning.

> "Okay, Adam is pounding on his desk. Let's all stop what we're doing and help Adam with his frustration . . ."
>
> "Okay, Amy, I gather from you're rolling your eyes that you don't agree?"
>
> These are just some of the techniques I used; that's probably enough for now.

Before you go on to the next section, do the **One Minute Inventory** on the next page.

Review: The One Minute Inventory

Ask yourself the following questions to evaluate your current skills as a facilitator.

1. Are you giving good instructions, explaining the purpose of exercises as well as the mechanics?

2. Are you clear and to the point? Are you using understandable language?

3. Are you maintaining a challenging but comfortable pace for learning?

4. Are you helping participants build upon each other's ideas and keeping class discussions lively with good questions?

5. Are you using flipcharts effectively to capture participants' comments?

6. Are you demonstrating the ability to listen and maintaining regular eye contact?

7. Are you managing the discussion to bring out key points and keeping participants motivated?

8. Are you using appropriate language (i.e. nonsexist, nonracist)?

9. Are your presentations well-organized?

10. Are you using body language and voice modulation to enhance your delivery?

11. Are you supportive and helpful to participants?

12. Can you deal effectively with difficult situations?

13. Are you able to help participants see the relationships between various course activities? Are you making the course relevant to their jobs?

14. Are you giving positive feedback on the group's progress? Both individually and to the whole group?

15. Do you respect the experiences and perceptions of participants?

It might be a good idea to keep referring to this page as you practice your delivery.

EXECUTE!

Enough information for you? Are you just itching to figure out what to do with it? Now's your chance to practice. You could say you've done all the programming there is; now it's time to apply what you learned.

Principles for promoting change

Every facilitator would like participants to accept new, worthwhile ideas and internalize them. To do this through training means introducing ideas in such a way that participants feel those ideas are an extension of their own goals. Participants will then demonstrate specific behaviors related to each new idea and maintain those behaviors on their own.

The following guidelines should help you achieve more acceptance and application of new ideas in your workshop sessions.

Principle I

Individuals are most likely to internalize new strategies when they are dissatisfied with their present practices. In other words, people are most open to change in areas that they have expressed interest in or a desire for more knowledge. They are least likely to accept change in areas in which they are satisfied with their performance.

Practical applications:

1. At the beginning of your workshop session, ask participants to identify areas they would like to know more about. Refer to this information as often as you can during your workshop. Point out references and connections and suggest additional articles, books, etc. at the end of the workshop.

2. During your session, give participants choices about the areas they will work on. These choices should be based on their suggestions as well as your observations. When individuals have an opportunity to decide which goal to pursue they are usually willing to invest the time and energy to support that decision. Don't simply dictate target areas.

> I had planned to spend most of the session on relaxation techniques. As
> the session unfolded, I found that the nurses wanted to develop safe places
> in which to vent their frustration. So I had to change my timetable in
> response to their concerns.

Principle II

Strategies that can be demonstrated are internalized at a higher rate than those that are simply explained or discussed.

Practical applications:

1. Demonstrate a new technique. Don't simply talk about it. Take time to demonstrate in as realistic a way as possible, using participant's work situation, how a new idea, behavior, or process works.

2. Make sure you and your participants have the same interpretation of the strategy. Do not assume that the other person's interpretation is the same as yours. Have participants voice their understanding of the new technique, idea, or behavior. Continue clarifying until everyone has the same interpretation. Have them demonstrate the method via role playing prior to trying it in the work setting.

3. Use practice and discussion frequently during your session. Incorporate techniques into your design that will allow participants to practice and observe new procedures.

Principle III

The type and amount of feedback participants receive directly affects the degree to which they internalize a new behavior or idea. It is important for participants to believe they are making progress in their learning. They need encouragement along the way.

Practical applications:

1. Feedback should be given on a regular basis throughout the session.

2. Use feedback to compliment individual and group's progress. Sometimes we focus on the negative and take the positive for granted. Feedback should be stated in positive rather than negative terms. Give individuals alternatives instead of mentioning only what went wrong. For example, it is more constructive to say, "I think it would help if you talked a little softer," than to say, "You talk too loud."

3. Ask individuals to evaluate their use of a new strategy and to give themselves feedback. Encourage each person to identify their areas of strength as well as those needing improvement. By identifying their own areas of strength, participants are likely to continue the positive behaviors they achieve.

4. Feedback should be specific, not general. A poor example would be, "You make other people feel uncomfortable." This type of response doesn't give the individual any specific behaviors to work on. The person may also be confused about what you mean by the word uncomfortable. A better response would be, "It is hard for people to approach you when you look mad and like you're about to blow up. It might be helpful if you learned to calm down."

Following these guidelines will take more time than simply telling people what to do. Yet in the long run, lasting change is more likely to happen.

Feedback as a communication skill

Feedback is similar to the questions and listening skills we have just described but is often more intense and focused. Feedback is not criticism!

For example, "I like the way you summarized the ideas about using the ACB model for attitude changing. Although I understand how you plan to do this when not on the job, I am unsure how you would use it during an actual stressful situation. Could you be more specific on a moment-to-moment basis?"

The first statement reinforces a strong point about what the facilitator did or said. The second one requires clarification of an important point. Both statements emphasize a response to what was said or done rather than accusing the speaker of doing something wrong.

There are some specific, helpful ways to express feedback:

- **As a clarification, summary, or question:** "What I heard you say was . . . "

- **As an observation:** "While I was speaking about . . . , I saw you sitting with your arms tightly folded. That signaled to me that you may not be comfortable with what I was saying."

- **As an expression of a feeling you had:** "When you said that, I became angry."

Here are some very basic rules for expressing feedback. Feedback is:

- **Either informational or behavioral.** It shows that you understand something, or it expresses how you feel about what someone said or did.

> "I guess I'm not too comfortable with what you said about your relationship with the orderlies. And they look about ready to erupt . . . "

- **Always specific.** It identifies exactly what it was you experienced, what you thought the other person said or did, or the way you feel.

> "Amy, when you said 'I can't do this,' I got the feeling you just didn't want to. Is there something about the exercise you're not comfortable with?"

- **Always directed at the issue or the behavior in question.** It is never directed at the character or personality of the other person. It is the difference between, "I think that doing that could be dangerous," versus, "You dummy! That is dangerous."
- **Always supportive.** Good feedback recognizes the other person's dignity even when you would like them to change a behavior that is adversely affecting you or the group.
- **Given only if the other person is ready and willing to accept it.**
- **Always given if it is requested.**
- **Accepted as such.** There is no obligation on your part to defend yourself or to return feedback for feedback.

> I found in my session that giving feedback rarely ended the problem-solving process. It usually began it, albeit effectively.
>
> That's the extent of the advice. Now you can review the summary and then complete your own action plan. You're as ready to facilitate a program as you can be!

Summary: Stand and Deliver

If you learned anything from this chapter, it must be clear that a boring or uninspired delivery can send all your planning out the window. It is your responsibility to channel the program towards a productive destination—the eyes, ears, minds, and hearts of your participants.

In order to successfully accomplish this, you must:

- recognize the significance of the relationship between yourself and your learners.

- create a positive learning environment where communication is encouraged and growth is the goal.

- identify the problems you face in order to determine solutions for those problems.

- use a variety of communication techniques and constantly examine your own abilities and limitations.

The pitfalls and barriers to effective communication are many, but knowing what they are is more than half the battle. The ability to recognize them as they arise will give you confidence in handling them. Thanks to Ruth and our lessons, you can handle them.

There are so many styles to emulate and borrow from. The best advice, though, is to find your own. Use what we have given you as an inventory that you may select from, to create your own identity as a trainer.

Visual aids are a part of any learning situation whether you want them to be or not. The fact is, if you don't give participants clear visual aids to help them retain information, they will be looking at you; then the signals you give in your facial expressions become the only visual aids you have!

Feedback is very important for participants. It is the communicative equivalent of tests and quizzes; it allows participants the chance to evaluate their statements and actions through your understanding of them.

▮▭▭▭▷ Action Plan

Remember: Set yourself up for success by choosing attainable goals. Start with small steps, especially in areas that are difficult for you. Become better at things you do well, then begin to move toward the unfamiliar. Proceed slowly and let yourself gain understanding as you go along. Know where you started from and give yourself credit for the progress you've made. Then say, "I can learn this, I am learning this, and I am doing well at this stage."

Promise to congratulate and reward yourself every time you accomplish something, no matter how small, to maintain and improve your adult learning skills.

I am proficient at these things, and I can do them more often:

1. _____

2. _____

3. _____

I have learned:

1. _____

2. _____

3. _____

My short-term goals for the above items are as follows:

1. _____

2. _____

3. _____

My long-term goals for the above items are as follows:

1. _____

2. _____

3. _____

Conclusion

In this manual, we've attempted to cover situations and aspects of training which are important to all trainers, from novices to those with years of experience. We hope it enlightened you to some new aspects of training or helped dust off one or two skills that had been tucked away in the corner of your mind. Perhaps it accomplished both.

Though it might seem that you now have an overwhelming amount of information to process, remember that you don't have to incorporate it all at once. Start with what you feel to be most important and incorporate it into your training sessions. As you see improvements and become more comfortable and confident, add others.

Photocopy the worksheets in the back of this book and use them to help you refine your skills.

This is Ruth signing off! I hope you will get as much satisfaction from helping people learn and change as I do.

References

Visualizing Facilitating the Adult Learner

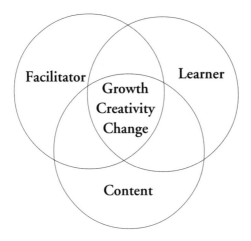

The Facilitator
- Sets environment
- Presents information

Who and what is an adult learner?

How do they learn new skills, ideas, concepts, etc.?

The Learner
- Characteristics
- Needs

What do adult learners need to know?

What facts, processes and/or information do I, the designer, choose?

The Content
- Information
- Skills
- Processes

The Learner + The Content + The Facilitator = Growth & Creativity & Change

L + C + F = New ideas, skills, processes (NiSP)

The Success-Goals are accomplished where the three come together in harmony.

Chart: The Adult Learner

The Teaching-Learning Process

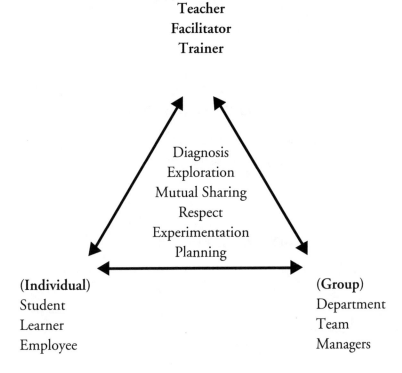

Teacher
Facilitator
Trainer

Diagnosis
Exploration
Mutual Sharing
Respect
Experimentation
Planning

(Individual)
Student
Learner
Employee

(Group)
Department
Team
Managers

The quality of this interdependent relationship directly determines the value and worth of the learning.

The ultimate question:

Has the learning experience been incorporated into the individual's life experience so they are better able to deal with some work or life problem?

Summary: Characteristics of the Adult Learner

SELF DIRECTED

They decide what is most important to learn!

EXPERIENCED BASED

They identify with what can be connected to,
or associated with, their life experiences.

MOTIVATED INTERNALLY

They respond to learning that enhances their self-esteem and self-confidence.

PROBLEM CENTERED

They seek and learn information that relates to real-life problems.

CAL = SEMP

Chart: Adult Learning Styles

	Feel	Watch	
Experience	Perceivers	Observers	Reflect
Question	Feelers	Thinkers	Evaluate
	Get involved	Theorize	

Chart

Adults have decisions to make and problems to solve.

If they want pure learning for learning's sake, there are many educational opportunities that offer such experiences; if they want pure entertainment, they can watch TV or go to a movie. Yet, when they seek educational experiences to enhance their performance on the job, they want help in real problem solving, decision-making, and skill building.

Adults do need a break from the demands of the job, however, and programs should be entertaining and enjoyable as well as problem-centered.

Ideal Conditions

Trainer/Facilitator	Materials	Participant
	have ↓	
has → → →	responsibility	← ← ← has
	↓	
needs to → → →	participate	← ← ← needs to
	↓	
must be able to → → →	create openness	← ← ← must be able to
	↓	
encourage → → →	support experimentation	← ← ← needs to
	↓	
will want to → → →	provide fun/work	← ← ← will want to
	↓	
must be → → →	sensitive to each individual in the group	← ← ← need to be

Each element creates the conditions conducive to a successful learning experience.

Remember!

All learning objectives need to contain the following:

Desired Behavior (Performance)	+	Under What Circumstance (Conditions)	±	Accepted Level of Accomplishment Standards	= Objectives
Behaviors Skills Knowledge		Description Situation		Norm Yardstick Measure	What is to be accomplished and how well under what conditions.
#1 What		#2 When		#3 How well	

Examples: Using the objectives for this segment . . .

Given previously selected materials, by the end of this workshop (#2 condition), be able to apply the principles of good program design (#1 performance), as set up by the facilitator (#3 standards).

In preparation for each training session you conduct (#2 condition), be able to select the appropriate visual aids to support your material (#1 performance), determined by the standards set in the design/development workshop and current design guides (#3 condition).

Describing Participants

What information do they need from me?

_____

_____

_____

_____

_____

What rewards will be important to them for coming?

_____

_____

_____

_____

What background skills do they bring to the program?

_____

_____

_____

_____

Questions I need to ask to help me better understand these participants:

_____

_____

_____

_____

_____

Describing Participants' Learning Goals

Review your notes on the previous worksheet and any other information about your future participants that you may need to include. In this section, you will further specify your participants' learning goals.

Now fill out the following worksheet as specifically as you can. The more thoroughly you can describe what your participants need and want to know, the more accurate your program goals will be. Also, consider management requests and your own expertise as you decide what to include in your program.

1. What do you feel that your participants really need to know? (These are their learning goals and will eventually be molded into your performance goals.)

_____

_____

_____

2. Does management have any additional goals that need to be included and are not covered above?

_____

_____

_____

3. What do you believe is important for your participants to learn?

_____

_____

_____

4. If these goals conflict, which are most important? Can they all be reached to some extent?

_____

_____

_____

✏️➡ Peformance Goals for Session: _____

After the session is complete:

Learners will know:

_____

_____

Attainment of this goal will be measured by:

_____

_____

Learners will feel:

_____

_____

Attainment of this goal will be measured by:

_____

_____

_____

Learners will do:

_____

_____

_____

Attainment of this goal will be measured by:

_____

_____

_____

✏️ Program Outline

Session: _____

Performance goal _____

1. _____

2. _____

3. _____

4. _____

5. _____

Performance goal _____

1. _____

2. _____

3. _____

4. _____

5. _____

Performance goal _____

1. _____

2. _____

3. _____

4. _____

5. _____

 **Preparation**

Questions and points to consider

1. Is there anything participants need to bring to your program?
2. Is advance preparation necessary for participants?
3. If participants need to bring supplies or complete pre-work, send them an announcement letter ten days to two weeks in advance.
4. Make sure directions are clear, and include a phone number the participants can call if they have questions.
5. Include the time, place, and date of the program, as well as any other essential instructions.

Information for your announcement

Welcome to (workshop title) _____

It will be held on (date) _____

from (starting and ending times) _____

The workshop location is (address/building/room, as needed) _____

_____

Directions to location (if needed) _____

_____

Prior to the session, please prepare by (reading, listing, etc.) _____

_____

Bring to the session (workbook, notepad, etc.) _____

_____

For more information, contact _____

at (phone #) _____

▬▬▬▶ Participant List

If at all possible, obtain a list of participants. Think about the kind of information you need to personalize your program and ask for it. If you will be offering other programs for the same groups, you may want to develop a paper or card file with a record for each participant or enter information in a computer database program.

Use the following outline, adding any information that will be important for you. Consider updating the file after the program is complete, particularly if you expect to see the participants again. Be sure to record the programs each person has attended.

Name: _____

Telephone number: _____

Company: _____

Job title: _____

Department: _____

Other information: _____

_____

_____

_____

_____

Program 1 / date: _____

Program 2 / date: _____

Program 3 / date: _____

Notes: _____

_____

_____

_____

◼▭▭▭▷ **Materials List**

This list will let you organize the material you actually use during your program. Fill it out now, but come back to it after you have read the resource guide at the end of this chapter.

Program name: _____

Leader's resources: _____

_____

_____

_____

_____

Teaching materials:

Slides; overheads; computer software, files, and handouts (name/number of copies)

_____

_____

_____

_____

_____

Equipment: easel/paper/markers; white board/markers; overhead projector; slide projector; screen; computer, etc.: _____

_____

_____

_____

_____

_____

✏️ Program Objectives

While you have already filled out something similar to this in Lesson 3, you may want to restate it here as a double check and reminder.

Program name: _____

By the end of this program, participants will be able to:

1. _____

_____

_____

2. _____

_____

_____

3. _____

_____

_____

4. _____

_____

_____

5. _____

_____

_____

✏️ Program Description

How would you concisely describe your workshop to someone who knows nothing about the topic?

_____

_____

_____

_____

_____

_____

Who is it for?

_____

_____

_____

_____

_____

_____

Are there any prerequisites?

_____

_____

_____

_____

_____

_____

Program Content Outline

Program title: _____

Segment 1: _____

_____

_____

_____

Segment 2: _____

_____

_____

_____

Segment 3: _____

_____

_____

_____

Segment 4: _____

_____

_____

_____

Segment 5: _____

_____

_____

_____

Agenda Notes

Program title: _____

Start	End	Segment
_____	_____	_____
_____	_____	_____
_____	_____	_____
_____	_____	_____
_____	_____	_____
_____	_____	_____
_____	_____	_____
_____	_____	_____
_____	_____	_____
_____	_____	_____
_____	_____	_____
_____	_____	_____
_____	_____	_____
_____	_____	_____
_____	_____	_____
_____	_____	_____
_____	_____	_____

✏️➤ Facilitator's Guide: Introduction Notes

Program title: _____

Opening statement: _____

_____

_____

_____

_____

_____

_____

Review of objectives: _____

_____

_____

Participant goals: _____

_____

_____

Outline for program with scheduled times: _____

_____

_____

Norms: _____

_____

_____

Housekeeping items: _____

_____

Facilitator's Guide: Program Notes

Major points	Training devices	Notes
_____	_____	_____
_____	_____	_____
_____	_____	_____
_____	_____	_____
_____	_____	_____
_____	_____	_____
_____	_____	_____
_____	_____	_____
_____	_____	_____
_____	_____	_____
_____	_____	_____
_____	_____	_____
_____	_____	_____
_____	_____	_____
_____	_____	_____
_____	_____	_____
_____	_____	_____
_____	_____	_____
_____	_____	_____
_____	_____	_____

✏️ Facilitator's Guide: Visual Notes

Visual title: _____

Source: _____

Storage location: _____

Used in programs/segments:

_____

_____

_____

_____

_____

_____

_____

_____

Main points to be made with visual:

_____

_____

_____

_____

_____

_____

_____

_____

➤ Facilitator's Guide: Worksheet Notes

Program name: _____

Segment: _____

Worksheet title: _____

Main points to be made with this worksheet:

_____

_____

_____

_____

_____

_____

_____

Describe the worksheet:

_____

_____

_____

_____

_____

_____

_____

_____

_____

_____

Facilitator's Guide: Conclusion Notes

Goal for conclusion:

_____

_____

_____

Process:

_____

_____

_____

Concluding statement:

_____

_____

_____

_____

_____

_____

_____

_____

_____

_____

_____

_____